DESIRING GOD
DVD STUDY GUIDE

A 12-part study of the classic book DESIRING GOD

by JOHN PIPER

DESIRING GOD
DVD STUDY GUIDE

Finding Complete Satisfaction and Joy in God

MULTNOMAH
BOOKS

DESIRING GOD DVD STUDY GUIDE
PUBLISHED BY MULTNOMAH BOOKS
12265 Oracle Boulevard, Suite 200
Colorado Springs, Colorado 80921

ISBN 978-1-60142-312-2

Published in the United States by WaterBrook Multnomah, an imprint of the Crown
Publishing Group, a division of Random House Inc., New York.

MULTNOMAH and its mountain colophon are registered trademarks of Random
House Inc.

Printed in the United States of America
2011—First Edition

10 9 8 7 6 5 4 3 2 1

SPECIAL SALES
Most WaterBrook Multnomah books are available at special quantity discounts when
purchased in bulk by corporations, organizations, and special-interest groups. Custom
imprinting or excerpting can also be done to fit special needs. For information, please
e-mail SpecialMarkets@WaterBrookMultnomah.com or call 1-800-603-7051.

Note: Page references in the book *Desiring God* cited in this study guide correspond to
the paperback edition published in 2011.

CONTENTS

INTRODUCTION
TO THIS STUDY GUIDE

Living a life of hedonism, in most people's minds, is the furthest thing from Christian obedience. The idea of seeking maximum pleasure in everything you do sounds like the epitome of selfishness and the absence of all self-control. For many, to live like a hedonist means to become an enemy of love and to set yourself in outright opposition to God.

But could this aversion to hedonism be an overreaction? In other words, could it be that we have allowed the concept of pursuing pleasure to be commandeered by the world and thereby lose any healthy sense of the idea for ourselves? After all, was not pleasure God's intention for man from the very beginning, when he filled Eden with "every tree that is pleasant to the sight and good for food" (Genesis 2:9) and gave Adam and Eve sexuality without shame (see Genesis 2:25)?

It is true. God did make us to enjoy pleasure, and not only in the garden. Throughout the Bible, God is calling his people to pursue pleasure and to pursue it in him. "Come, everyone who thirsts, come to the waters; and he who has no money, come, buy and eat!" (Isaiah 55:1). "If anyone thirsts, let him come to me and drink" (John 7:37). "Rejoice in the Lord always; again I will say, Rejoice" (Philippians 4:4).

The tragedy of sin is that it sidetracks and shortchanges us of the real joy of knowing God. Satan offers stolen goods, which are indeed sweet, but the span is short, and the cost far outweighs the benefits. God, on the other hand, extends far sweeter and infinitely longer-lasting pleasures: "In your presence there is *fullness* of joy; at your right hand are pleasures *forevermore*" (Psalm 16:11). True hedonism, *Christian* hedonism, sees God as the source of the best delights and is unashamed to forsake sin and follow hard after him.

The aim of this study guide and its accompanying DVD is to help you see that God-hungry hedonism is biblically acceptable. On top of that, it argues that such hedonism is not merely one more option for how to follow God but must instead be the fuel and fervor that motivates and empowers *all* of your obedience. Finally, this study seeks to highlight several of the ways laid out in Scripture for cultivating and increasing such desire and delight in God.

This study guide is designed to be used in a twelve-session* guided group study that focuses on the *Desiring God* DVD set.[1] After an introductory lesson, each subsequent lesson examines one thirty-minute session[2] from the *Desiring God* DVD set. You the learner are encouraged to prepare for the viewing of each session by reading and reflecting upon Scripture, by considering key quotations, and by asking yourself penetrating questions. Your preparatory work for Lessons 2–11 is marked with the heading "Before You Watch the DVD, Study and Prepare."

The workload is conveniently divided into five daily, manageable assignments. There is also a section suggesting further study. This work is to be completed individually before the group convenes to view the DVD and discuss the material.

> Throughout this study guide, paragraphs set off and printed in this typeface are excerpts from a book written by John Piper or excerpts taken from the Desiring God Web site (www.desiringgod.org). They are included to supplement the study questions and to summarize key or provocative points.

The second section in Lessons 2–11, entitled "Further Up and Further In," is designed for the learner who wants to explore in greater detail the concepts and ideas introduced in the lesson. This section is not required, but it will deepen your understanding of the material. This section requires that you read online sermons or articles from the Desiring God Web site (www.desiringgod.org) and answer relevant questions. These sermons can be found by performing a title search at the Desiring God Web site.

The third section in Lessons 2–11, entitled "While You Watch the DVD, Take Notes," is to be completed as the DVD is playing. This section includes fill-in-the-blanks and leaves space for note taking. You are encouraged to engage with the DVD by filling in the appropriate blanks and writing down other notes that will aid you during the group discussion.

The fourth section in each normal lesson is "After You Watch the DVD, Discuss What You've Learned." Three discussion questions are provided to guide and focus the conversation. You may record, in the spaces provided, notes that will help you contribute to the conversation. Or you may use this space to record things from the discussion that you want to remember.

The fifth and final section is an application section: "After You Discuss, Make Application." You will be challenged to record a takeaway point and to engage in a certain activity that is a fitting response to the content presented in the lesson.

Group leaders will want to peruse the Leader's Guide, which is included at the conclusion of the study guide.

Life transformation will only occur by the grace of God. Therefore, we highly encourage you to seek the Lord in prayer throughout the learning process. Pray that God would open your eyes to see wonderful things in his Word. Pray that he would grant you the insight and concentration you need in order to get the most from this resource. Pray that God would cause you to not merely understand the truth, but also to rejoice in it. And pray that the discussion in your group would be mutually encouraging and edifying. We've included objectives at the beginning of each lesson. These objectives won't be realized without the gracious work of God through prayer.

---

*While this study guide is ideally suited for a twelve-session study, it is possible to complete it in six sessions. For instructions on how to use this study guide for a six-session group study, turn to Appendix A, "Six-Session Intensive Option."

INTRODUCTION TO *DESIRING GOD*

LESSON OBJECTIVES

It is our prayer that after you have finished this lesson...

- You will have a better sense of how you and others in your group approach the Christian life.
- Your thoughts on the subject will be stirred, and questions will come to mind.
- You will grow more eager to hear what the Bible says about the essence of following Christ.

ABOUT YOURSELF

1. What is your name?
2. Tell the group something about yourself that they probably don't already know.
3. What are you hoping to learn from this study?

A PREVIEW OF *DESIRING GOD*

1. In one sentence write your personal mission statement that answers the question "What is my overarching purpose in life?" Share your statement with the group and explain how you arrived at it.

2. List what you think are the top five virtues in the Christian life and rate them from one to five, with one being the most important. Share your list and ratings with the group and explain your reasoning.

ONE GREAT MISSION AND MOTIVATION

A Companion Study to the Desiring God DVD, Session 1

LESSON OBJECTIVES

It is our prayer that after you have finished this lesson...
- You will have a biblical sense of the overarching purpose of your life.
- You will understand and love the essence of God's commands.
- You will see how crucial the issue of motivation is in the Christian life.

⟶ *Before You Watch the DVD, Study and Prepare* ⟵

DAY 1—THE BIG PICTURE

The concepts presented in this study are big. They challenge the very core of our view of God, our view of ourselves, and our understanding of the essence of the Christian life. Therefore, in preparation to engage with these great themes, it is good for us to begin turning our minds—with Scripture as our guide—in the direction we will be heading.

The Westminster Shorter Catechism, written in England in the seventeenth century, is a work designed to summarize and teach the great doctrines of the Christian faith. It begins with the huge and simple question, "What is the chief end of man?" and answers, "Man's chief end is to glorify God, and to enjoy him forever."

* **Question 1:** If you were asked, "What is the chief end of man?" what would you say? What passages of Scripture might inform your answer?[3]

Now consider the end of the book of Ecclesiastes. After twelve chapters of contemplating the meaning of life and the purposes of man, the author concludes with these words in Ecclesiastes 12:13–14:

[13]The end of the matter; all has been heard. Fear God and keep his commandments, for this is the whole duty of man. [14]For God will bring every deed into judgment, with every secret thing, whether good or evil.

Question 2: What, according to the author of Ecclesiastes, should be your chief end? How does this compare with the Westminster Shorter Catechism or your answer to question 1? Why does the author of Ecclesiastes think this question is so important?

DAY 2—ALL TO THE GLORY OF GOD

In the previous section we saw that the author of Ecclesiastes considers the whole duty (or "chief end") of man to be "Fear God and keep his commandments." He does not list out the specific commandments he has in mind but only states the principle.

Jesus, in Matthew 22:36–40, takes the author of Ecclesiastes' principle and explains that the commands (1) to love God with all of your heart, soul, and mind, and (2) to love your neighbor as yourself encapsulate every other command. Therefore love to God and love to others, according to Jesus, is the way in which we "keep [God's] commandments."

Like Jesus, Paul also explains what the ultimate aim of Christian obedience should be. But he puts it in different words in 1 Corinthians 10:31:

> [31]So, whether you eat or drink, or whatever you do, do all to the glory of God.[4]

* **Question 3:** What do you think it means to "do all to the glory of God"? For instance, what does eating or drinking to God's glory look like? And what difference is there—if any—between Paul's way of talking about Christian obedience and Christ's?

By saying, "whatever you do," Paul applies the command "do all to the glory of God" to every single area of life. Whether homework or yard work, parenting or paintballing, hygiene or hospitality, Paul implies that every aspect of our existence can be carried out in a God-glorifying way.

Question 4: List five specific, even mundane, activities that are a part of your day-to-day life (such as driving to work or washing the dishes). Then write a sentence or two next to each one describing how it might be done to the glory of God.

Day 3—Head Toward the Heart

We have already seen that, according to Ecclesiastes 12, the whole duty of man is to "fear God and keep his commandments." We have also identified Paul's summary of all of God's commandments in the phrase "do all to the glory of God," and we sought to explain and apply what this might mean for our day-to-day lives. Now, before we go any further, we have reached a good place to pause and consider how our hearts are responding to these first two sections.

> **Question 5:** How does the fact that you have a duty to "fear God and keep his commandments" strike you? Is it a relief to have such a purpose? Or does it make you feel burdened? Try to be as honest as you can and explain your answer.

Now listen to the words of 1 John 5:3–4:

> ³For this is the love of God, that we keep his commandments. And his commandments are not burdensome. ⁴For everyone who has been born of God overcomes the world. And this is the victory that has overcome the world—our faith.

> * **Question 6:** Notice in verse 3 that John equates keeping God's commandments with loving him. How might keeping God's commandments be equal to loving him? In verse 3, John also states that God's commandments are not burdensome. What reason does he give for this in verse 4?

Day 4—Duplicity Does Not Help

We took some time in the previous section to tend to our hearts. This is important because, although outwardly we may seem to be obeying God and growing in our knowledge of him, this may not always be the case internally.

An illustration of this kind of discontinuity between our outsides and insides is found in 1 Samuel 16:6–7. After God rejected Saul as king over Israel, he sent Samuel to Bethlehem to anoint one of Jesse's sons as the new king. Upon his arrival, Samuel invites Jesse and his sons to meet him.

> 6 When they came, [Samuel] looked on Eliab and thought, "Surely the LORD's anointed is before him." 7 But the LORD said to Samuel, "Do not look on his appearance or on the height of his stature, because I have rejected him. For the LORD sees not as man sees: man looks on the outward appearance, but the LORD looks on the heart."

Although outwardly Eliab appeared to be well suited for the kingship, inwardly there was something about his heart that made him an unfit candidate. Samuel could not see it, but God could, and on account of that he had already rejected him.

* **Question 7:** What does the fact that "the LORD looks on the heart" imply about the nature of true obedience?

One part of life in which people are particularly susceptible to being different on the outside than they are on the inside—that is, hypocritical—is in religion. That was the case with the Pharisees in Jesus' day, the most outwardly devout people in all of Israel. Listen to what he had to say to them in Matthew 23:25–28:

²⁵Woe to you, scribes and Pharisees, hypocrites! For you clean the outside of the cup and the plate, but inside they are full of greed and self-indulgence. ²⁶You blind Pharisee! First clean the inside of the cup and the plate, that the outside also may be clean.

²⁷Woe to you, scribes and Pharisees, hypocrites! For you are like whitewashed tombs, which outwardly appear beautiful, but within are full of dead people's bones and all uncleanness. ²⁸So you also outwardly appear righteous to others, but within you are full of hypocrisy and lawlessness.

Question 8: Why do you think religious people are more prone to hypocrisy? How can a Christian identify his or her hypocrisy?

Day 5—Love Must Lead You

We saw in 1 Samuel that God is not fooled by outward appearances but looks on the heart, as was the case with Eliab, Jesse's son. This was also the case with the people of Israel in Isaiah's day. Through the prophet, God says of them in Isaiah 29:13:

¹³This people draw near with their mouth and honor me with their lips, while their hearts are far from me.

Question 9: Restate this verse in your own words. Can you think of an example of this kind of behavior in your own life? If so, describe.

Perhaps the most vivid description of the tragedy of neglecting the heart when it comes to Christian obedience is found in 1 Corinthians 13:1–3:

> ¹If I speak in the tongues of men and of angels, but have not love, I am a noisy gong or a clanging cymbal. ²And if I have prophetic powers, and understand all mysteries and all knowledge, and if I have all faith, so as to remove mountains, but have not love, I am nothing. ³If I give away all I have, and if I deliver up my body to be burned, but have not love, I gain nothing.

* **Question 10:** According to this passage, why is it so important to take note of the motivations behind our actions? What do you think is ultimately at stake with this issue? (See Matthew 7:21–23 for further consideration.)

Further Up and Further In

Note: The "Further Up and Further In" section is for those who want to study more. It is a section for further reference and going deeper. The phrase "further up and further in" is borrowed from C. S. Lewis.

As noted in the introduction, each lesson in this study guide provides the opportunity for you to do further study. In this section, you will have the opportunity to read a sermon or article and answer some questions about what you read.

Read or listen to "The Joyful Duty of Man," an online sermon at the Desiring God Web site.

> **Question 11:** What does John Piper say it means to glorify God? How does this compare with your answer to question 3 above?

> **Question 12:** Piper uses four examples to illustrate how man's duty to glorify God is not a burdensome task. How would you summarize the argument that he is making with these examples?

Read the article "We Want You to Be a Christian Hedonist!" on the Desiring God Web site.

> **Question 13:** The term *hedonist* is controversial for some people because of the worldly connotations it most often carries. How does Piper define "*Christian* hedonism," and how does he distinguish it from worldly hedonism?

> **Question 14:** What is Piper's response to the statement made by some people that duty should be our main motivation, not delight?

Question 15: Toward the end of the article Piper states, "It is never a problem to want to be satisfied. The problem is being satisfied too easily." Do you agree with this statement? Why or why not? How does Piper distinguish satisfaction that comes easy from that which is more difficult to attain?

—→ *While You Watch the DVD, Take Notes* ←—

John Piper says that the topic of Christian hedonism is both

_____ and _____.

According to Piper, what is the summary of the book *Desiring God*?

The Bethlehem Baptist Church mission statement says, "We exist
   to spread a _____ for the _____
   of God in all things for the _____ of all peoples
   through _____."

Commenting on Luke 14:13–14, T. W. Manson says that to live for
   the sake of reward is to live in what way?

What does Immanuel Kant say is necessary in order for an action
   to be moral?

—→ *After You Watch the DVD, Discuss What You've Learned* ←—

1. What is it about Christian hedonism that Piper says makes it
    both devastating and liberating? What is your initial response
    to it?

2. Piper gave a little autobiography about his "struggle with moti-
    vation." What made the issue of motivation a struggle for him?
    Can you relate to him in this?

3. Ayn Rand was not convinced by Immanuel Kant's ethic, nor
    is Piper. Why did they disagree with him? Do you agree with
    their critiques? If so, do you see *any* truth in Kant's claim?

—•→ *After You Discuss, Make Application* ←•—

1. What was the most meaningful part of this lesson for you? Was
    there a sentence, concept, or idea that really struck you? Why?
    Record your thoughts in the space below.

2. Take a moment this coming week to read through Matthew
    6:1–18. What incentives does Jesus provide for the kind of giv-
    ing, praying, and fasting that he describes? Spend time medi-
    tating on these incentives and praying that they would move
    you to obey God.

A SUMMARY OF CHRISTIAN HEDONISM

A Companion Study to the Desiring God *DVD, Session 2*

LESSON OBJECTIVES

It is our prayer that after you have finished this lesson...
- You will see that to desire your own happiness is not in itself a bad thing.
- You will affirm that the highest possible happiness is having God.
- You will acknowledge the importance of joy in the Christian life.

—→ *Before You Watch the DVD, Study and Prepare* ←—

DAY 1—DEFENDING DESIRE

In the previous lesson, Ayn Rand and John Piper took issue with Immanuel Kant over his understanding of Christian morality. C. S. Lewis likewise had trouble with Kant's conclusion:

If there lurks in most modern minds the notion that to desire our own good and earnestly to hope for the enjoyment of it is a bad thing, I submit that this notion has crept in from Kant and the Stoics and is no part of the Christian faith. Indeed, if we consider the unblushing promises of reward and the staggering nature of the rewards promised in the Gospels, it would seem that Our Lord finds our desires not too strong, but too weak.[5]

* **Question 1:** Why, according to Lewis, is Kant's notion or morality "no part of the Christian faith"? When Lewis mentions "rewards promised in the Gospels," can you think of one or two that he may have had in mind?

Take a look at this word from God in Isaiah 55:1–3:

[1]Come, everyone who thirsts, come to the waters; and he who has no money, come, buy and eat! Come, buy wine and milk without money and without price. [2]Why do you spend your money for that which is not bread, and your labor for that which does not satisfy? Listen diligently to me, and eat what is good, and delight yourselves in rich food. [3]Incline your ear, and come to me; hear, that your soul may live; and I will make with you an everlasting covenant, my steadfast, sure love for David.

Question 2: What kinds of desire is God appealing to in this passage? Does this passage support or contradict what Lewis said above?

Day 2—What About Sin?

If we agree with what we have already heard from Piper, Rand, and Lewis that the desire to be happy should not be considered *in itself* a bad thing, then what are we to make of James 1:14–15?

> [14]But each person is tempted when he is lured and enticed by his own desire. [15]Then desire when it has conceived gives birth to sin, and sin when it is fully grown brings forth death.

> * **Question 3:** James 1:14–15 clearly says that sin comes from a person's desire. Do these verses support the claim that all desiring is evil, including the desire to be happy? Explain why or why not.

The best way to understand (as much as possible) what an author's words mean is to read them in context. So before making any final conclusions on James 1:14–15, we should consider his additional comments on desire just three chapters later, in James 4:1–2:

> [1]What causes quarrels and what causes fights among you? Is it not this, that your passions are at war within you? [2]You desire and do not have, so you murder. You covet and cannot obtain, so you fight and quarrel. You do not have, because you do not ask.

Question 4: At first glance it appears that James is again faulting desire for sins, specifically here the sins of quarrelling, fighting, and murdering. But what reason does he give for why the people's passions (desires) are resulting in sin? Do these verses give you any insight into what determines whether desire turns into sin (James 1:14–15) or leads us to God (Isaiah 55:1–3)?

I don't assume that renunciation goes with submission or even that renunciation is good in itself. Always you renounce a lesser good for a greater; the opposite is what sin is.... The struggle to submit...is not a struggle to submit but a struggle to accept and with passion. I mean, possibly, with joy. Picture me with my ground teeth stalking joy—fully armed too as it's a highly dangerous quest.[6]

DAY 3—THE BEST SOUL FOOD

What we noticed in Isaiah 55:1–3 (Day 1) was that God was appealing to his people's hunger and thirst: "Come, everyone who *thirsts*, come to the waters; and he who has no money, come, buy and *eat!*"

But we also saw that God was speaking in metaphors. The feasting he had in mind was not ultimately upon physical food: "Incline your ear, and come to me; hear, that your *soul* may live; and I will make with you *an everlasting covenant, my steadfast, sure love for David.*"

And so the Lord says it plainly: the cravings of his people are cravings in their *soul,* and the answer to those cravings is his covenant *love.*

* Question 5: In what ways does your soul hunger and thirst?
What does it long to have? How might the covenant love of
God satisfy those longings?

The psalms talk a lot about the soul-satisfying goodness of God.
Here are a few examples where the psalmist is speaking directly to God:

[7]You have put more joy in my heart than they have when their
grain and wine abound. (Psalm 4:7)

[11]You make known to me the path of life; in your presence there is
fullness of joy; at your right hand are pleasures forevermore.
(Psalm 16:11)

[3]Because your steadfast love is better than life, my lips will praise
you. (Psalm 63:3)

[25]Whom have I in heaven but you? And there is nothing on earth
that I desire besides you. [26]My flesh and my heart may fail, but
God is the strength of my heart and my portion forever. (Psalm
73:25–26)

Question 6: One way the psalmists express their regard for God
and the satisfaction that he gives is by comparing him to other
things. What are some of the things these verses compare God
to, and how do they measure up?

Day 4—Compounding the Pleasure

The psalmists are not the only people in Scripture who express their pleasure in God. The apostles likewise testify to their joy in him. For example, John says:

> ¹That which was from the beginning, which we have heard, which we have seen with our eyes, which we looked upon and have touched with our hands, concerning the word of life— ²the life was made manifest, and we have seen it, and testify to it and proclaim to you the eternal life, which was with the Father and was made manifest to us— ³that which we have seen and heard we proclaim also to you, so that you too may have fellowship with us; and indeed our fellowship is with the Father and with his Son Jesus Christ. ⁴And we are writing these things so that our joy may be complete. (1 John 1:1–4)

Through the gospel the apostles had come to experience the joy of having fellowship "with the Father and with his Son Jesus Christ." And John writes this letter so that his readers also "may have fellowship with us." This sounds very thoughtful of John to be sharing the gospel out of such concern for the good of others. But notice that he does not end there. In verse 4 he mentions another motive behind his writing to them: "so that our joy may be complete."

* **Question 7:** How might the act of sharing the gospel with other people increase John's own joy in it? Is this experience something peculiar to John or the gospel message, or can you think of anything else that becomes better when you share it with others?

John delighted to share the gospel with others. He also delighted to see people persevere in believing it.

> ²Beloved, I pray that all may go well with you and that you may be in good health, as it goes well with your soul. ³For I rejoiced greatly when the brothers came and testified to your truth, as indeed you are walking in the truth. ⁴I have no greater joy than to hear that my children are walking in the truth. (3 John 2–4)

Question 8: How do you suppose John's joy became so intertwined with the spiritual and physical well-being of others? Are you like him in this regard? If not, how might you become more like him?

DAY 5—IS JOY JUST EXTRA?

The simple fact that God made us is reason enough for all people to give themselves entirely to him. He owns us, not to mention that he sent his Son to die for us and to deal with our sins. So what does it matter that following God can be a delightful thing? It seems secondary to the fact that it is simply our duty.

The author of Hebrews, however, suggests that the desirability of God to us is a more important factor than that.

> ⁶And without faith it is impossible to please him, for whoever would draw near to God must believe that he exists and that he rewards those who seek him. (11:6)

* **Question 9:** According to this verse, what two things must a person with faith believe? Why do you think God makes it necessary for us to believe these things about him?

Consider the following paragraph by John Piper.

Christian Hedonism teaches that the desire to be happy is God-given and should not be denied or resisted but directed to God for satisfaction. Christian Hedonism does not say that whatever you enjoy is good. It says that God has shown you what is good and doing it ought to bring you joy (Micah 6:8). And since doing the will of God ought to bring you joy, the pursuit of joy is an essential part of all moral effort. If you abandon the pursuit of joy (and thus refuse to be a Hedonist, as I use the term), you cannot fulfill the will of God.... According to Christian Hedonism joy in God is not optional icing on the cake of Christianity. When you think it through, joy in God is an essential part of saving faith.[7]

Piper argues that "doing the will of God ought to bring you joy," and to support his claim, he quotes Micah 6:8:

[8]He has told you, O man, what is good; and what does the LORD require of you but to do justice, and to love kindness, and to walk humbly with your God?

Question 10: How does Micah 6:8 support Piper's conclusion that joy is a necessary part of Christian obedience? After thinking it through, do you find that you are in agreement with Piper? Why or why not?

FURTHER UP AND FURTHER IN

Read or listen to "Worship: The Feast of Christian Hedonism," an online sermon at the Desiring God Web site.

Question 11: How does Piper define worship in the first two sections, and what are the three ways that our hearts can respond in worship to God?

Question 12: Further down Piper posits and answers four objections to Christian hedonism. In dealing with the second objection, what does Piper identify as the key to not killing joy or worship?

Question 13: Toward the end of his response to the fourth objection, Piper alludes to the first answer from the Westminster Shorter Catechism (see Lesson 2, Day 1), and he offers a slight revision. What is the revision that Piper recommends, and how does it change the meaning?

Read the article "'Fact! Faith! Feeling!'" on the Desiring God Web site.

Question 14: What have people traditionally used the phrase "Fact, Faith, Feeling" to signify? What two potential problems does Piper see with such usage?

Question 15: Piper thinks it is right that, at conversion, people accept Christ as both Lord and Savior. He writes, however, that something is still missing from that description. What, in Piper's mind, is missing, and why does he think it is so important?

—◆ *While You Watch the DVD, Take Notes* ◆—

A Summary of Christian Hedonism in Five Statements
1. The longing to be happy is a _____ human experience, and it is _____, not _____.

2. We should never try to _____ or _____
   our longing to be happy, as though it were a bad impulse.
   Instead we should seek to _____ this long-
   ing and _____ it with whatever will provide
   the deepest and most enduring satisfaction.

3. The deepest and most enduring satisfaction is found

   _____.

4. The happiness we find in God reaches its consummation when
   it expands to meet the _____
   in the manifold ways of love.

5. To the extent we try to abandon the pursuit of our own pleasure, we fail to _____ and
   _____. Or, to put it positively: the
   pursuit of pleasure is _____
   of all worship and virtue.

→⋆ *After You Watch the DVD, Discuss What You've Learned* ⋆←

1. Blaise Pascal said that all men seek happiness, even those who
   hang themselves. Do you agree with him? What exceptions
   can you name, if any?

2. Piper said that the solution to our tendency to sin is not to kill
   all desire but to glut ourselves on God. Think of a particular
   sin in your life that you would be willing to share with the
   group. In what ways would glutting yourself on God outdo the
   pleasure you get from that sin?

3. True Christian hedonism, according to Piper, maximizes its joy
    when it reaches out in love to meet the needs of others. Are
    there currently any needs among the people in your family,
    church, or community that are not being met? If so, how
    might you as an individual or a discussion group reach out to
    bless and be blessed?

—✷ *After You Discuss, Make Application* ✷—

1. What was the most meaningful part of this lesson for you? Was
    there a sentence, concept, or idea that really struck you? Why?
    Record your thoughts in the space below.

2. Make a list of three aspects of worship or virtuous living that
    you do not always enjoy. Each day this week pray that God
    would enable you to delight in him and in these activities.

THE FOUNDATION OF CHRISTIAN HEDONISM

A Companion Study to the Desiring God *DVD, Session 3*

LESSON OBJECTIVES

It is our prayer that after you have finished this lesson...
- You will understand that God is indomitably happy.
- You will see that his happiness is ultimately in his own glory.
- You will discern in Scripture that God's glory is the aim of all that he does.

→ *Before You Watch the DVD, Study and Prepare* ←

DAY 1—GAUGING GOD'S HEART

In the previous lessons we examined the human heart and its motivations. In this lesson we shall consider *God's* heart and *his* motivations.

Question 1: Preliminary survey: From what you know right now, what would you say God values most highly? Give it some thought and write down what you come up with, citing any relevant verses you can think of.

We will come back to this answer. But before we go any further, perhaps we should ask whether or not God actually *is* happy. Then we can better determine what it is that *makes* him happy.

Consider the following word from Nebuchadnezzar:

[34]At the end of the days I, Nebuchadnezzar, lifted my eyes to heaven, and my reason returned to me, and I blessed the Most High, and praised and honored him who lives forever, for his dominion is an everlasting dominion, and his kingdom endures from generation to generation; [35]all the inhabitants of the earth are accounted as nothing, and he does according to his will among the host of heaven and among the inhabitants of the earth; and none can stay his hand or say to him, "What have you done?" (Daniel 4:34–35)

* **Question 2:** According to this text, what are some possible arguments for saying that God is a happy God? If these things are true, can you think of anything that would prevent God from being happy?

Think about it for a moment: If God is sovereign and can do anything He pleases, then none of His purposes can be frustrated.... And if none of His purposes can be frustrated, then He must be the happiest of all beings. This infinite, divine happiness is the fountain from which the Christian Hedonist drinks and longs to drink more deeply.[8]

DAY 2—GOD PRIZES WHAT HE PURSUES

"Our God is in the heavens; he does all that he pleases" (Psalm 115:3). Piper says that if this verse is true, then God must be "the happiest of all beings." Nothing and no one can keep him from doing what he wants. His sovereignty guarantees him unceasing satisfaction.

Yet the question remains: What does God *do* that makes him happy? What does he exert his sovereignty *for*? "The way to answer this question," says Piper, "is to survey what God pursues in all His works. If we could discover what one thing God pursues in everything He does, we would know what He delights in most. We would know what is uppermost in His affections."[9]

> * **Question 3:** From your present knowledge of the Scriptures, can you think of any one thing that God consistently pursues in everything he does? (Remember: You must consider what he does not only in his acts of kindness and redemption but also in his acts of judgment and wrath.) Write down any thoughts or passages that come to mind.

There is a clue in the great doxology of Romans 11 for what God's ultimate goal might be.

[33]Oh, the depth of the riches and wisdom and knowledge of God! How unsearchable are his judgments and how inscrutable his ways! [34]"For who has known the mind of the Lord, or who has been his counselor?" [35]"Or who has given a gift to him that he might be repaid?" [36]For from him and through him and to him are all things. To him be glory forever. Amen. (vv. 33–36)

Question 4: What does Paul attribute to God in these verses? What does he say returns back to God in the end?

DAY 3—EXAMINING THE EXODUS

When testing to see if an idea is biblical or not, it is best to first ask whether it comes from the Bible itself or if it is something conceived of outside the text. Although ideas conceived of on the outside may at times still be compatible with Scripture and conceptually true, it is certainly the case that those stated explicitly in the Bible are much easier to ascertain and accept.

We suggested in the last section that the goal to which God does "all things" in Romans 11:36 is for his own glory: "To him be *glory* forever. Amen." But we must ask: Is this the clear testimony of Scripture?

There are other Desiring God resources that list dozens of passages in support of this claim[10]—including the forthcoming DVD session— but for our purposes here, it will be best to focus on only a select few. Take, for instance, what Scripture says about the Exodus:

[17]And I will harden the hearts of the Egyptians so that they shall go in after them, and I will get glory over Pharaoh and all his host, his chariots, and his horsemen. [18]And the Egyptians shall know that I am the LORD, when I have gotten glory over Pharaoh, his chariots, and his horsemen. (Exodus 14:17–18)

* **Question 5:** From what you see in this passage, why did God harden the hearts of the Egyptians and drown their army in the Red Sea? What does it mean to "get glory" over someone?

Defeating the Egyptians was not the only way God fulfilled his purposes in the Exodus.

7Our fathers, when they were in Egypt, did not consider your wondrous works; they did not remember the abundance of your steadfast love, but rebelled by the sea, at the Red Sea. 8Yet he saved them for his name's sake, that he might make known his mighty power. (Psalm 106:7–8)

Question 6: How did God respond to his people's rebellion at the Red Sea, and why did he respond the way he did? What does "for his name's sake" mean? Do you see any similarities between this passage and Exodus 14:17–18 above?

The term *glory of God* in the Bible generally refers to the visible splendor or moral beauty of God's manifold perfections. It is an attempt to put into words what cannot be contained in words—what God is like in His unveiled magnificence and excellence.

Another term that can signify much the same thing is the *name of God.* When Scripture speaks of doing something "for God's name's sake," it means virtually the same as doing it "for His glory."[11]

Day 4—What the Prophets Taught

Another section of Scripture that gives us insight into the heart of God is the Old Testament prophets. In his book, Isaiah proclaims to the people of Israel why God has remained faithful and merciful to them, even though they have not been faithful to him:

> [9]For my name's sake I defer my anger, for the sake of my praise I restrain it for you, that I may not cut you off. [10]Behold, I have refined you, but not as silver; I have tried you in the furnace of affliction. [11]For my own sake, for my own sake, I do it, for how should my name be profaned? My glory I will not give to another. (48:9–11)

> **Question 7:** Circle the phrases above that express God's purposes in his actions toward Israel. What do these phrases suggest about God's values and priorities?

The book of Ezekiel also opens a window for us into the heart of God. In response to his people's sin, God prophesies through Ezekiel that he is going to make a new covenant with them, an "everlasting covenant" (Ezekiel 37:26). But why? It is worth quoting his entire answer.

> [22]Therefore say to the house of Israel, Thus says the Lord God: It is not for your sake, O house of Israel, that I am about to act, but for the sake of my holy name, which you have profaned among the nations to which you came. [23]And I will vindicate the holiness of my great name, which has been profaned among the nations, and which you have profaned among them. And the nations will

know that I am the LORD, declares the Lord GOD, when through you I vindicate my holiness before their eyes. ²⁴I will take you from the nations and gather you from all the countries and bring you into your own land. ²⁵I will sprinkle clean water on you, and you shall be clean from all your uncleannesses, and from all your idols I will cleanse you. ²⁶And I will give you a new heart, and a new spirit I will put within you. And I will remove the heart of stone from your flesh and give you a heart of flesh. ²⁷And I will put my Spirit within you, and cause you to walk in my statutes and be careful to obey my rules. ²⁸You shall dwell in the land that I gave to your fathers, and you shall be my people, and I will be your God. ²⁹And I will deliver you from all your uncleannesses. And I will summon the grain and make it abundant and lay no famine upon you. ³⁰I will make the fruit of the tree and the increase of the field abundant, that you may never again suffer the disgrace of famine among the nations. ³¹Then you will remember your evil ways, and your deeds that were not good, and you will loathe yourselves for your iniquities and your abominations. ³²It is not for your sake that I will act, declares the Lord GOD; let that be known to you. Be ashamed and confounded for your ways, O house of Israel. (Ezekiel 36:22–32)

* **Question 8:** In the other passages we have seen in this lesson, God states positively why he is acting: so that he will "get glory" or "for [his] name's sake." But here he clarifies his point by stating what is *not* his motivation. In the above passage, what is *not* motivating God to act? What are the implications of this for his people?

Because God is unique as an all-glorious, totally self-sufficient Being, He must be for Himself if He is to be for us.... If God should turn away from Himself as the Source of infinite joy, He would cease to be God. He would deny the infinite worth of His own glory. He would imply that there is something more valuable outside Himself. He would commit idolatry.[12]

Day 5—Problem Solving and Processing

One potential problem with claiming that God's greatest delight is himself is revealed by the following question: If God is perfectly satisfied in himself, then why did he ever make us?

What this question reveals is that when we say that God is most satisfied in his own glory as it is reflected back to him, we are in danger of suggesting that God has somehow made himself dependent on us. But consider these words of Paul to the men of Athens:

[24]The God who made the world and everything in it, being Lord of heaven and earth, does not live in temples made by man, [25]nor is he served by human hands, as though he needed anything, since he himself gives to all mankind life and breath and everything. (Acts 17:24–25)

* **Question 9:** According to this passage, for what is mankind dependent upon God? For what is God dependent upon mankind? Now compare these two. What effect should this comparison have on us?

Through all eternity God the Father has beheld the image of His own glory perfectly represented in the person of His Son. Therefore, one of the best ways to think about God's infinite enjoyment of His own glory is to think of it as the delight He has in His Son, who is the perfect reflection of that glory (John 17:24–26)....

In creation, God "went public" with the glory that reverberates joyfully between the Father and the Son. There is something about the fullness of God's joy that inclines it to overflow. There is an expansive quality to His joy. It wants to share itself. The impulse to create the world was not from weakness, as though God were lacking in some perfection that creation could supply. "It is no argument of the emptiness or deficiency of a fountain, that it is inclined to overflow."[13]

The answer this quote provides to our previous question is that the creation of the universe and of mankind was God's way of putting his own self-sufficiency and perfect satisfaction on display. The Father was already infinitely happy as he beheld the image of himself in his Son, and the tendency of that joy was simply to spill over.[14]

As we conclude our study for Lesson 4, we recognize that the idea that God loves his glory more than anything can be quite difficult to process, especially at first. For many of us, it upsets our prior conceptions of God, rubs against our moral sense, and sounds utterly foreign to what we have heard taught in church. This kind of response is usual and understandable. There are legitimate questions here that should not be brushed over lightly. But rest assured, there are answers.

For the time being, we simply encourage you to keep an open heart and mind, consider the Scriptures, pay attention as John Piper teaches from them, and give everything to God in prayer. "He leads the humble in what is right, and teaches the humble his way" (Psalm 25:9).

All my years of preaching and teaching on the supremacy
of God in the heart of God have proved that this truth
hits most people like a truck laden with unknown fruit. If
they survive the impact, they discover that this is the
most luscious fruit on the planet.[15]

Question 10: Where are you in this picture? Have you survived
the impact and started enjoying the fruit, or are you still in
critical condition? State and explain your status below.

Further Up and Further In

**Read or listen to "God Created Us for His Glory," an online sermon
at the Desiring God Web site.**

Question 11: What does Piper say are "two of the most important
questions for any human being to answer"? What reasons does
he give for why they are important?

Question 12: What can "for his glory" *not* mean, according to
Piper? How does he support this?

Read or listen to "How to Do Good So That God Gets the Glory," an online sermon at the Desiring God Web site.

> **Question 13:** According to Piper, what must be happening in our lives in order for God to get glory?

> **Question 14:** What clarification was Piper trying to make by titling this sermon the way that he did?

> **Question 15:** How does Piper answer the question "How do we serve or do good so that God gets the glory?"

―→ *While You Watch the DVD, Take Notes* ←―

The Six Stages of Redemptive History
   1. _____
Scripture passage:

   2. _____
Scripture passage:

   3. _____
Scripture passage:

4. _____

Scripture passage:

5. _____

Scripture passage: Philippians 1:9–11

6. _____

Scripture passage:

—→ *After You Watch the DVD, Discuss What You've Learned* ◆—

1. Toward the beginning of the video Piper says, "What I'm about to show you is so unsettling to the unregenerate soul that people get mad." Why do you suppose people who are not born again get angry when Piper teaches about these things?

2. As he begins his discussion of propitiation, Piper states that the cross of Christ is the center of the Savior's work and, indeed, all of history. How is God's greatest act, the death of Christ, particularly glorifying to God and not to man?

3. Survey each member of your study group: How are you handling this week's lesson? Are you finding it agreeable? surprising? upsetting? awesome? Why or why not? You might ask how you can pray for one another in this regard.

—➤ *After You Discuss, Make Application* ◆—

1. What was the most meaningful part of this lesson for you? Was there a sentence, concept, or idea that really struck you? Why? Record your thoughts in the space below.

2. What is it that makes God so glorious? That is, what is so great about him that he would be most enthralled with himself? List as many things that you can, ten at the least, along with any related Bible passages you can think of. You may wish to take a few minutes to pray through them, giving thanks and praising God for what he has revealed of himself to you.

THE ESSENCE OF CHRISTIAN HEDONISM

A Companion Study to the Desiring God *DVD, Session 4*

LESSON OBJECTIVES

It is our prayer that after you have finished this lesson...
- You will have a better understanding of the biblical definition of love.
- You will see that God positions himself as the greatest gift of love.
- You will know that you are loved the most when God loves God the most.

→ *Before You Watch the DVD, Study and Prepare* ←

DAY 1—DEFINING LOVE

One problem people often have with the idea that God is most passionate about his own glory is that it does not sound very loving.

Question 1: How do you think the average person defines love today? How do you define it? (Cite any passages of Scripture that inform your answer.) Is there a difference between the two? If so, explain.

How does the Bible define love? In Lesson 2 we learned from 1 John 5:3–4 that one way to define our love for God is that we keep his commandments. But that definition cannot work the other way around, because God doesn't receive commandments from us. So what might it mean for God to love us?

Paul makes it clear in Romans 5:8:

[8]God shows his love for us in that while we were still sinners, Christ died for us.

We see here that God defines his love for us by what he did at the cross: Christ *died* for us. "Greater love has no one than this, that someone lay down his life for his friends" (John 15:13). That is exactly what Christ did.

* **Question 2:** How can dying for someone be a loving thing? Applying it to the cross, how was Christ's death for us a loving thing? You may have several answers. List all below, including Scripture references.

Day 2—Love Gives Life

John 3:16 is probably the most familiar and straightforward answer to how Christ loved us by dying for us:

> [16]For God so loved the world, that he gave his only Son, that
> whoever believes in him should not perish but have eternal life.

By dying on the cross, Christ spared those of us who believe in him from death, from the just and eternal punishment of God's wrath against our sin. But he did more than that: he gave us eternal life!

Eternal life. But what is that? Life as it is right now, but without end? Or is it something entirely different than what we have ever experienced? Hear how Jesus clarifies this term in his high priestly prayer, just hours before going to the cross.

> [3]And this is eternal life, that they know you the only true God,
> and Jesus Christ whom you have sent. (John 17:3)

Question 3: What does Jesus say eternal life is? What do you think it means to know God and Jesus Christ?

From John 3:16 we see that Christ died in order that we might be delivered from death and given eternal life. And in John 17:3 we learn that eternal life means knowing God the Father and Jesus Christ his Son. The apostle Peter puts these two verses together for us and reaffirms in one sentence the essence of how God loved us through the cross, the most loving act he ever did.

[18]For Christ also suffered once for sins, the righteous for the unrighteous, that he might bring us to God. (1 Peter 3:18)

* **Question 4:** What does Peter say was Christ's purpose in giving his life for us? If the greatest way the Father could love us was by bringing us to himself through his Son, what does this say about God's presence?

In view of God's infinite power and wisdom and beauty, what would His love for a human being involve? Or to put it another way: What could God give us to enjoy that would prove Him most loving? There is only one possible answer: *Himself!* If He withholds Himself from our contemplation and companionship, no matter what else He gives us, He is not loving.[16]

DAY 3—IS GOD'S LOVE REALLY LOVING?

You may have noticed that in the previous two sections we did not address 1 Corinthians 13, although it is perhaps the most familiar passage in the Bible about what love is (and is not). We should look at it now.

[4]Love is patient and kind; love does not envy or boast; it is not arrogant [5]or rude. It does not insist on its own way [Greek: "It seeks not its own"]; it is not irritable or resentful; [6]it does not rejoice at wrongdoing, but rejoices with the truth.

Question 5: Looking at this description of love, list those aspects that you see demonstrated in Jesus' death on the cross and briefly explain beside each one how you see it demonstrated. Are there any aspects that you do not see at work on Calvary?

In light of what has already been shown about God's purposes in the cross—namely, that he struck down his Son in order to show his righteousness (see Romans 3:25–26) and bring us to him (see 1 Peter 3:18)—it might seem that God's love does, in fact, "seek...its own."

But is this truly the case? Do Paul's words in 1 Corinthians 13 really contradict such a view of God's love? Consider the following quote from Piper:

> God is the one Being in all the universe for whom seeking His own praise is the ultimately loving act. For Him, self-exaltation is the highest virtue. When He does all things "for the praise of His glory," He preserves for us and offers to us the only thing in all the world that can satisfy our longings. God is for us! And the foundation of this love is that God has been, is now, and always will be for Himself.[17]

* **Question 6:** How, according to Piper, is self-exaltation God's highest virtue? Why would it not be a virtue for us to imitate him and exalt ourselves?

DAY 4—MORE EVIDENCE: LAZARUS

We have seen from the past several sections that the evidence of God's love for us is that he sent his Son to die for us (see Romans 5:8). We saw how this was love, because, for those who believe in Jesus, it gives eternal life (see John 3:16), which means being with (see 1 Peter 3:18) and knowing (see John 17:3) God the Father and God the Son. Therefore God is not unloving to us if he exalts himself or loves himself most of all, because in doing that, he is, in fact, promoting our greatest eternal good: himself.

The cross of Christ, then, is a demonstration of love—indeed, the greatest demonstration of love that ever was—with the glory of God at the very center. Nonetheless, in order to show more convincingly that God's pursuit of his own glory is not at odds with love, it may help to look at a few more examples in Scripture:

> [1]Now a certain man was ill, Lazarus of Bethany, the village of Mary and her sister Martha. [2]It was Mary who anointed the Lord with ointment and wiped his feet with her hair, whose brother Lazarus was ill. [3]So the sisters sent to him, saying, "Lord, he whom you love is ill." [4]But when Jesus heard it he said, "This illness does not lead to death. It is for the glory of God, so that the Son of God may be glorified through it." [5]Now Jesus loved Martha and her sister and Lazarus. [6]So [Greek: "therefore"], when he heard that Lazarus was ill, he stayed two days longer in the place where he was. (John 11:1–6)

Question 7: What does this passage say was Jesus' disposition toward Lazarus and his sisters? What did he do after hearing that Lazarus was ill, and from what you know about the rest of the story, what was the initial effect of this on Lazarus?

It is possible to interpret these seemingly opposite realities—that is, that Jesus loved Lazarus and yet Lazarus died—as simply a result of Jesus not being able to get to him in time. In other words, Jesus was limited by the constraints of his human body and just could not make the journey soon enough. He loved Lazarus and did not intend for him to die, but the circumstances were such that his death was already inevitable. Therefore Jesus stayed where he was.

> * **Question 8:** Read John 11:1–6 again. Do you see any other
> options for why Jesus would have stayed? How might Jesus'
> love for Lazarus and God's desire to get glory both be accom-
> plished by Jesus' waiting and Lazarus's dying?

DAY 5—A FINAL EXAMPLE: JESUS' PRAYER

A third example of how God's passion for his glory is loving toward us, in addition to our examination of the cross and the story of Lazarus, comes from Jesus' words in John 17. As we noted back in Day 2 of this lesson, this chapter records Jesus' high priestly prayer, in which he prays for his disciples and for those who will believe in him through their Word. Here is how he begins:

> ¹When Jesus had spoken these words, he lifted up his eyes to
> heaven, and said, "Father, the hour has come; glorify your Son
> that the Son may glorify you, ²since you have given him authority
> over all flesh, to give eternal life to all whom you have given him.
> ³And this is eternal life, that they know you the only true God,
> and Jesus Christ whom you have sent. ⁴I glorified you on earth,
> having accomplished the work that you gave me to do. ⁵And now,

Father, glorify me in your own presence with the glory that I had with you before the world existed.

Question 9: As you read through these verses, underline the requests Jesus makes. What are they? Why might Jesus begin an extended prayer for his followers this way?

Another significant portion of this prayer to consider is the conclusion:

[24]Father, I desire that they also, whom you have given me, may be with me where I am, to see my glory that you have given me because you loved me before the foundation of the world. [25]O righteous Father, even though the world does not know you, I know you, and these know that you have sent me. [26]I made known to them your name, and I will continue to make it known, that the love with which you have loved me may be in them, and I in them. (John 17:24–26)

* **Question 10:** Why does Jesus want his people to be with him in heaven? Notice that twice in this passage Jesus mentions God's love for him, once specifying it as existing from "before the foundation of the world." Why do you think God loved Jesus from before the foundation of the world, and what do you think that kind of love would look like inside of you? (See verse 26.)

Further Up and Further In

Read or listen to "God Demonstrates His Love Toward Us," an online sermon at the Desiring God Web site.

Question 11: What four observations does Piper make about experiencing God's love? List them below.

Question 12: How does Piper define revival? Why does he say it is necessary from time to time?

Question 13: What two things does Piper say we can do in order to experience more of God's love?

Read the article "The Goal of God's Love May Not Be What You Think It Is" on the Desiring God Web site.

Question 14: According to Piper, what is the aim of true love? Why does he think this is so important?

Question 15: What does Piper say is a profoundly wrong way to handle the cross of Christ?

—➤ *While You Watch the DVD, Take Notes* ◆—

The essence of Christian hedonism: man's chief end is to glorify God _____ enjoying him.

C. S. Lewis said, "I think we delight to praise what we enjoy because the praise not merely expresses but _____ the enjoyment."[18]

According to Jonathan Edwards, "God is glorified not only by His glory's being _____, but by its being _____."[19]

If you want to test the love of God, don't ask the question, "Is he helping me _____?" Ask, "Am I able, through these _____, to see more of his _____?"

You sin because you _____. The solution to that is not, "I will no longer _____." The solution is (1) _____ and (2) _____.

—➤ *After You Watch the DVD, Discuss What You've Learned* ◆—

1. C. S. Lewis said that we delight to praise what we enjoy (such as good food, movies, music, etc.). Assuming he is right, why do you think this is the case?

2. Piper said that we should not measure the love of God by how many problems he helps us avoid but by the grace that he gives us in them. Recount a difficulty that the Lord has brought you through, and then share how you experienced his grace as a result.

3. If God's love consists in enabling us to enjoy (and thus glorify) him forever, what implications does this have for how we should love others? Can you give a concrete example of what this might look like?

—→ *After You Discuss, Make Application* ←—

1. What was the most meaningful part of this lesson for you? Was there a sentence, concept, or idea that really struck you? Why? Record your thoughts in the space below.

2. Is there a Bible verse or passage covered in this study that has been illumining or encouraging to you? See if you can commit it to memory. We recommend writing it down and putting it on your wall or in your pocket and then reviewing it daily for the next week. Scripture memory, as we shall see, is one of the best ways to fight for joy in God.

THE GRAND OBLIGATION (PART 1): COMMANDED TO REJOICE

A Companion Study to the Desiring God *DVD, Session 5*

LESSON OBJECTIVES

It is our prayer that after you have finished this lesson…

- You will be more aware of all the opportunities in the world for more joy in God.
- You will recognize the tendency in your own heart to settle for lesser pleasures.
- You will see that seeking greater joy in God is not an option but an obligation.

—➤ *Before You Watch the DVD, Study and Prepare* ◆—

DAY 1—WITNESSING GOD IN THE WORLD

Alongside seeing him in the Scriptures, another way to stir up joy in God is to see him in the world. The psalmist who wrote Psalm 104 gives us a glimpse into how he did this.

[10]You make springs gush forth in the valleys; they flow between the hills; [11]they give drink to every beast of the field; the wild donkeys quench their thirst. [12]Beside them the birds of the heavens dwell; they sing among the branches. [13]From your lofty abode you water the mountains; the earth is satisfied with the fruit of your work. [14]You cause the grass to grow for the livestock and plants for man to cultivate, that he may bring forth food from the earth [15]and wine to gladden the heart of man, oil to make his face shine and bread to strengthen man's heart. [16]The trees of the LORD are watered abundantly, the cedars of Lebanon that he planted. [17]In them the birds build their nests; the stork has her home in the fir trees. [18]The high mountains are for the wild goats; the rocks are a refuge for the rock badgers. [19]He made the moon to mark the seasons; the sun knows its time for setting. [20]You make darkness, and it is night, when all the beasts of the forest creep about. [21]The young lions roar for their prey, seeking their food from God. [22]When the sun rises, they steal away and lie down in their dens. [23]Man goes out to his work and to his labor until the evening. [24]O LORD, how manifold are your works! In wisdom have you made them all; the earth is full of your creatures.

* **Question 1:** What occurrences in the natural world does the psalmist attribute to God? Underline them in the passage above. After observing them, what does the psalmist conclude about God?

George Herbert, a seventeenth-century English poet and pastor, saw revelations of God's character in creation. In his poem "The Pulley" he observes how earthly riches tell of God's goodness but also serve a second purpose.

When God at first made man,
Having a glass of blessings standing by,
Let us (said he) pour on him all we can:
Let the world's riches, which dispersed lie,
Contract into a span.

So strength first made a way;
Then beauty flowed, then wisdom, honour, pleasure:
When almost all was out, God made a stay,
Perceiving that alone of all his treasure,
Rest in the bottom lay.

For if I should (said he)
Bestow this jewel also on my creature,
He would adore my gifts instead of me,
And rest in Nature, not the God of Nature:
So both should losers be.

Yet let him keep the rest,
But keep them with repining restlessness;
Let him be rich and weary, that at least,
If goodness lead him not, yet weariness
May toss him to my breast.

Question 2: What gift does Herbert say God has withheld from
man? Why does he think God withheld it? Do you think
Herbert is right?

Day 2—Corrupt Contentment

Even though God's glory can be seen in the Bible and in creation—and therefore there exists untold potential for our growth in joy as we give our attention to them both—it is, sadly, too often the case that we content ourselves with much smaller glories. C. S. Lewis saw and diagnosed this poor tendency of the human heart.

> We are half-hearted creatures, fooling about with drink and sex and ambition when infinite joy is offered us, like an ignorant child who wants to go on making mud pies in a slum because he cannot imagine what is meant by the offer of a holiday at the sea. We are far too easily pleased.[20]

> * **Question 3:** What is the reason, in Lewis's mind, for why people are prone to settle for lesser pleasures? What do you think is necessary in order to move beyond this?

In Ephesians 3, Paul prays for the church at Ephesus, asking that they might "know the love of Christ that surpasses knowledge," and "be filled with all the fullness of God" (verse 19). That sure sounds like seeing glory and having joy! What assurance does Paul give them that such a thing is even possible? Read the very next sentence:

> [20]Now to him who is able to do far more abundantly than all that we ask or think, according to the power at work within us, [21]to him be glory in the church and in Christ Jesus throughout all generations, forever and ever. Amen.

Question 4: Why do you think Paul would have closed his prayer with this benediction? How do statements of God's abilities and promises help us, in terms of Lewis's image, to move beyond mud pies and head toward the sea?

Day 3—Thou Shalt Be Happy

We must understand that the ability to be wholeheartedly happy in God is not just an option for Christians who are "more spiritual" to pursue. It is a matter of *obedience*. And it applies to *all* believers. Consider this sentence from 1 Thessalonians 5:

> [16]Rejoice always, [17]pray without ceasing, [18]give thanks in all circumstances; for this is the will of God in Christ Jesus for you.

> * **Question 5:** Why do you think it is God's will that believers "rejoice always"? How could that even be possible?

James, like Paul, similarly commanded his readers to rejoice. But rather than speaking in general about when they should rejoice, he got specific.

> [2]Count it all joy, my brothers, when you meet trials of various kinds, [3]for you know that the testing of your faith produces steadfastness. [4]And let steadfastness have its full effect, that you may be perfect and complete, lacking in nothing. (James 1:2–4)

Question 6: What reason does James give for why we should be able to rejoice in the midst of trials? Try to think of a trial that you faced recently. Were you able to rejoice in it? If not, what prevented you from rejoicing?

Day 4—Exult or Else

The necessity that we rejoice in him is so great that God does not stop at commanding it. He issues threats to those who will not obey.

> [47]Because you did not serve the Lord your God with joyfulness and gladness of heart, because of the abundance of all things, [48]therefore you shall serve your enemies whom the Lord will send against you, in hunger and thirst, in nakedness, and lacking everything. And he will put a yoke of iron on your neck until he has destroyed you. (Deuteronomy 28:47–48)

* **Question 7:** Can threats like this be loving? Why or why not? If so, how might this one be loving?

In case a person should think that such threats only occur in the Old Testament, let us look at Jesus' words to the church in Ephesus from Revelation 2.

> [2]I know your works, your toil and your patient endurance, and how you cannot bear with those who are evil, but have tested

those who call themselves apostles and are not, and found them to be false. [3]I know you are enduring patiently and bearing up for my name's sake, and you have not grown weary. [4]But I have this against you, that you have abandoned the love you had at first. [5]Remember therefore from where you have fallen; repent, and do the works you did at first. If not, I will come to you and remove your lampstand from its place, unless you repent.

It is abundantly clear from verse 5 that Jesus is using the threat of removing the Ephesians' lampstand (which, as we see in Revelation 1:20, is their status as a church) as a way to motivate them.

> **Question 8:** What is Jesus wanting the Ephesians to do? Notice that works are present in their current status (Revelation 2:1), just as they were in the past (2:5), but now something is missing: love. What is the difference between works done in love to Christ and works done without it?

Suppose a husband asks his wife if he must kiss her good night. Her answer is, "You must, but not that kind of a must." What she means is this: "Unless a spontaneous affection for my person motivates you, your overtures are stripped of all moral value."[21]

Day 5—The Essence of Evil

If what we have seen so far is true, then we can now affirm that neglecting to seek joy in God is disobedience for any Christian. More than that, it is dangerous, because God delivers judgment upon those who will not delight in him. One further thing our study reveals is that the failure to pursue satisfaction in God is not just disobedient and dangerous; it is the very essence of evil.

> [12]Be appalled, O heavens, at this; be shocked, be utterly desolate, declares the LORD, [13]for my people have committed two evils: they have forsaken me, the fountain of living waters, and hewed out cisterns for themselves, broken cisterns that can hold no water. (Jeremiah 2:12–13)

* **Question 9:** What are the two evils God identifies in verse 13? Restate them in your own words. Why would he call them evil?

A passage from the New Testament that expresses the same thing is James 4:3–4:

> [3]You ask and do not receive, because you ask wrongly, to spend it on your passions. [4]You adulterous people! Do you not know that friendship with the world is enmity with God? Therefore whoever wishes to be a friend of the world makes himself an enemy of God.

Question 10: What do you think James means by "friendship with the world"? What effect does he say it has on our relationship with God?

FURTHER UP AND FURTHER IN

Read or listen to "True Christianity: Inexpressible Joy in the Invisible Christ," an online sermon at the Desiring God Web site.

> **Question 11:** Why, as Piper understands it, does Peter tell his readers what they are experiencing?

> **Question 12:** How does Piper define "joy in Christ"? How does he differentiate this from "loving Christ" and "trusting Christ"?

> **Question 13:** Why is it, according to Piper, that with our Bibles we are in a better position to rejoice in Christ than the people who lived around him when he was on earth?

Read the article "Treating Delight as Duty Is Controversial" on the Desiring God Web site.

> **Question 14:** From Piper's experience, what is one reason people find Christian hedonism so controversial?

Question 15: What kind of happiness does Piper say Christians are "duty-bound to pursue"?

—➤ *While You Watch the DVD, Take Notes* ◄—

God has two books:
1.
2.

What is the main question Piper sets out to answer in this segment?

Argument 1:

Argument 2:

Argument 3:

—➤ *After You Watch the DVD, Discuss What You've Learned* ◀—

1. In the beginning of this session Piper talks about the world as the theater of God. In what ways do you see God in the world? Remember: Piper said that God is not evident only in the natural order, but also in the social, political, and cultural spheres.

2. C. S. Lewis said that our problem with desiring God is that we are far too easily pleased with other things to care about having greater joy. Think about your situation and that of Christians where you live. What lesser pleasures do you see stifling the further growth of your joy in God?

3. If, as Piper's third argument states, the essence of evil is forsaking the joy that God offers and seeking satisfaction elsewhere, what implications does this have for how Christians should pursue holiness in this life?

—*→ *After You Discuss, Make Application* ←*—

1. What was the most meaningful part of this lesson for you? Was there a sentence, concept, or idea that really struck you? Why? Record your thoughts in the space below.

2. We all struggle with putting other joys in this life above our joy in God, and, as Piper said, most of these are innocent idols. Examine your heart. What might be your biggest idol? Write it down, along with some practical ideas for how you can replace the pleasure it gives you with pleasure in God.

THE GRAND OBLIGATION (PART 2): AN ESSENTIAL ELEMENT OF FAITH AND WORSHIP

A Companion Study to the Desiring God *DVD, Session 6*

LESSON OBJECTIVES

It is our prayer that after you have finished this lesson…
- You will understand that Scripture issues commands to our emotions.
- You will see that joy is an essential part of true conversion and ongoing faith.
- You will recognize that God is most glorified in us when we are most satisfied in him.

→ *Before You Watch the DVD, Study and Prepare* ←

DAY 1—DOES LOVE INVOLVE EMOTION?

Some people reject the notion that we are obligated to enjoy God because they say it is not possible to control emotions, and God would not command us to do something we cannot control. We have seen, however, that there are numerous commands in Scripture for us to be glad in God.

How about love? We know that it is clearly commanded throughout Scripture. But does love involve our emotions (or affections, as they are sometimes called)? Let us revisit Revelation 2:2–5, which we first covered in Day 4 of Lesson 6.

> [2]I know your works, your toil and your patient endurance, and how you cannot bear with those who are evil, but have tested those who call themselves apostles and are not, and found them to be false. [3]I know you are enduring patiently and bearing up for my name's sake, and you have not grown weary. [4]But I have this against you, that you have abandoned the love you had at first. [5]Remember therefore from where you have fallen; repent, and do the works you did at first. If not, I will come to you and remove your lampstand from its place, unless you repent.

Question 1: What did you learn about love from this passage? Do you think the love that Jesus commands here requires emotion? Why or why not?

Consider what Paul says of love in his letter to the Romans.

> [9]Let love be genuine. Abhor what is evil; hold fast to what is good. [10]Love one another with brotherly affection. Outdo one another in showing honor. (12:9–10)

* **Question 2:** What do you think Paul means by "brotherly affection"? If it does, in fact, signify emotions that we cannot control, why might Paul feel justified in commanding it anyway?

DAY 2—ENJOINING THE EMOTIONS

A short examination of the Bible reveals that emotions of all types are regu-
larly commanded by God throughout the Old and New Testaments.

> [1]Be not envious of evil men, nor desire to be with them, [2]for
> their hearts devise violence, and their lips talk of trouble.
> (Proverbs 24:1–2)

* **Question 3:** What is Solomon commanding *not* to happen in
these verses? Restate his words positively below. Would you say
he is commanding emotions? Defend your answer.

Sometimes God gives his commands in the form of prohibitions,
such as the Ten Commandments. "You shall not covet your neighbor's
house" (Exodus 20:17). Other times he gives them positively, such as
with the Golden Rule: "So whatever you wish that others would do to
you, do also to them" (Matthew 7:12). And sometimes he uses negative
and positive together:

³But sexual immorality and all impurity or covetousness must not even be named among you, as is proper among saints. ⁴Let there be no filthiness nor foolish talk nor crude joking, which are out of place, but instead let there be thanksgiving. (Ephesians 5:3–4)

Question 4: What does Paul see as the root behind sinful speech? What is its opposite? Would you classify either of these as emotions? Explain.

Day 3—The Nature of Faith

A further argument for the necessity of joy in the Christian life is the biblical evidence that joy is an essential part of saving faith.

How would you define faith? Of those who are familiar with the New Testament, many would probably turn first to Hebrews 11:1.

¹Now faith is the assurance of things hoped for, the conviction of things not seen.

Question 5: In the case of Christian faith, what are these "things hoped for" and "not seen"? List the first few that come to your mind. How does this verse relate to Hebrews 11:6 (Lesson 3, Day 5)?

Observe how Jesus spoke about saving faith:

[37]On the last day of the feast, the great day, Jesus stood up and cried out, "If anyone thirsts, let him come to me and drink. [38]Whoever believes in me, as the Scripture has said, 'Out of his heart will flow rivers of living water.'" [39]Now this he said about the Spirit, whom those who believed in him were to receive, for as yet the Spirit had not been given, because Jesus was not yet glorified. (John 7:37–39)

* **Question 6:** Why do you think Jesus would use the analogy of thirsting and drinking in his invitation to people to believe in him? What does this passage suggest about the role of the Holy Spirit in the life of a believer?

Day 4—Joy in Conversion

If, as we saw in the previous section, delight in God is an essential part of saving faith, how does this affect our understanding of what happens at conversion?

Scripture suggests that conversion, in large part, consists of being awakened to enjoy God's glory.

[19]And I will give them one heart, and a new spirit I will put within them. I will remove the heart of stone from their flesh and give them a heart of flesh, [20]that they may walk in my statutes and keep my rules and obey them. And they shall be my people, and I will be their God. (Ezekiel 11:19–20)

* Question 7: What do you think God means by the term "heart of flesh"? What is true of those who have one?

Listen to what Jesus had to say about why some are *not* converted:

¹⁹And this is the judgment: the light has come into the world, and people loved the darkness rather than the light because their works were evil. ²⁰For everyone who does wicked things hates the light and does not come to the light, lest his works should be exposed. (John 3:19–20)

Question 8: What reasons does Jesus give for why unbelievers do not come to the light? What does this imply about those who *do* come?

Day 5—God Is Praised When He Is Prized

The final argument in this lesson for the indispensable role of joy in the Christian life is that God cannot be glorified in all things by any other way.

¹⁸ᵇYes, and I will rejoice, ¹⁹for I know that through your prayers and the help of the Spirit of Jesus Christ this will turn out for my deliverance, ²⁰as it is my eager expectation and hope that I will not

be at all ashamed, but that with full courage now as always Christ
will be honored in my body, whether by life or by death. (Philippians 1:18b–20)

Question 9: Why is Paul confident that he will go on rejoicing?
What does he mean by "my deliverance"?

In the second half of the paragraph, Paul grounds what he has just
said in verse 20:

[21]For to me to live is Christ, and to die is gain. [22]If I am to live in
the flesh, that means fruitful labor for me. Yet which I shall
choose I cannot tell. [23]I am hard pressed between the two. My
desire is to depart and be with Christ, for that is far better.

* **Question 10:** According to Paul, how will Christ be magnified in
his life? How so in his death? Write down any additional
observations from this passage.

FURTHER UP AND FURTHER IN

**Read or listen to "Love One Another with Brotherly Affection," an
online sermon at the Desiring God Web site.**

Question 11: How does Piper describe the kind of love that we should have for one another in the church?

Question 12: What are the four reasons, according to Piper, for why it is important to love one another with brotherly affection?

Question 13: What three practical things does Piper highlight to help you grow in your love for other believers?

Read the article "On the Possibility of Saying 'I Love You, but I Don't Like You'" on the Desiring God Web site.

Question 14: What are Piper's two problems with Joseph Fletcher's premise that "feelings cannot be commanded"?

Question 15: What practical reason does Piper give for not buying Fletcher's conclusion that "love is not liking"?

—•» *While You Watch the DVD, Take Notes* «•—

Piper continues to make the case that pursuing joy in God is essential to Christian obedience. He adds four more arguments in this lesson (although you will notice that he switches the order of number 4 and number 5).

Argument 5:
Scripture cited:

Argument 4:
Scripture cited:

Argument 6:
Scripture cited:

Argument 7: Praising God (Worship) Is, in Essence, Prizing God
Scripture cited: Philippians 1:19–23

—•» *After You Watch the DVD, Discuss What You've Learned* «•—

1. Think back to the time when you first came to know the Lord. What effect did that experience have on you emotionally?

2. Do you consider yourself an emotional or passionate person? How do you feel about Piper's claim that obedience to God requires us to have certain emotions?

3. Romans 12:15 says, "Rejoice with those who rejoice, weep with those who weep." How can a person who doesn't typically experience much emotion obey this command?

—❧ *After You Discuss, Make Application* ❧—

1. What was the most meaningful part of this lesson for you? Was there a sentence, concept, or idea that really struck you? Why? Record your thoughts in the space below.

2. One gift God has given us to help grow our affections for him is prayer. Take a few minutes to write a prayer to God, making it as short or long as you wish. One possibility would be to write a prayer of thanksgiving that you could use at mealtimes.

THE GRAND OBLIGATION (PART 3): HOLY HEDONISM IS LOVE

A Companion Study to the Desiring God *DVD, Session 7*

LESSON OBJECTIVES

It is our prayer that after you have finished this lesson…

- You will realize that joy is essential to keeping the command to love.
- You will understand how the pursuit of pleasure leads to sacrificial giving.
- You will recognize this kind of pleasure-seeking love in action throughout the Bible.

--→ *Before You Watch the DVD, Study and Prepare* ←--

DAY 1—MIMIC THE MACEDONIANS

Jesus is clear: to love God and to love our neighbor are the two greatest commandments (see Matthew 22:37–40). Therefore, we must ask whether the call to pursue our joy in God ultimately fulfills them.

Read 2 Corinthians 8:1–8:

¹We want you to know, brothers, about the grace of God that has been given among the churches of Macedonia, ²for in a severe test of affliction, their abundance of joy and their extreme poverty have overflowed in a wealth of generosity on their part. ³For they gave according to their means, as I can testify, and beyond their means, of their own accord, ⁴begging us earnestly for the favor of taking part in the relief of the saints— ⁵and this, not as we expected, but they gave themselves first to the Lord and then by the will of God to us. ⁶Accordingly, we urged Titus that as he had started, so he should complete among you this act of grace. ⁷But as you excel in everything—in faith, in speech, in knowledge, in all earnestness, and in our love for you—see that you excel in this act of grace also. ⁸I say this not as a command, but to prove by the earnestness of others that your love also is genuine.

Question 1: What does Paul commend to the Corinthians as a sign of genuine love from the churches of Macedonia? What caused this kind of love from them?

One chapter later Paul draws out what was so admirable among the Macedonians, and he applies it directly to the Corinthians.

⁷Each one must give as he has decided in his heart, not reluctantly or under compulsion, for God loves a cheerful giver. (2 Corinthians 9:7)

* **Question 2:** According to Paul, what matters most when it comes to giving? If God loves a cheerful giver, what do you think is his disposition toward those who are not cheerful?

DAY 2—PROFITABLE PASTORING

On Day 1 we observed from the Macedonians what genuine love looks like in the context of giving, particularly in their case from one church to another. But what does love look like within churches, between the sheep and their pastors?

> ²Shepherd the flock of God that is among you, exercising oversight, not under compulsion, but willingly, as God would have you; not for shameful gain, but eagerly. (1 Peter 5:2)

Question 3: According to this verse, what are some bad reasons for pastors to do their jobs? In your own words, how would you describe the better way for them to shepherd their people?

Now consider what Scripture says about how congregations should behave toward their pastors:

> ¹⁷Obey your leaders and submit to them, for they are keeping watch over your souls, as those who will have to give an account. Let them do this with joy and not with groaning, for that would be of no advantage to you. (Hebrews 13:17)

* **Question 4:** Why should a congregation care if its pastor is groaning? How can congregations help their pastors have joy?

Day 3—It Is More Blessed to Give

In Acts 20:17–38 Paul is on the seashore at Miletus, saying good-bye and giving final instructions to the Ephesian elders who had come to see him off. In his parting address, Paul warns them against pastoring for the sake of worldly gain and points to his own example.

> [33]I coveted no one's silver or gold or apparel. [34]You yourselves know that these hands ministered to my necessities and to those who were with me. [35]In all things I have shown you that by working hard in this way we must help the weak and remember the words of the Lord Jesus, how he himself said, "It is more blessed to give than to receive." (Acts 20:33–35)

* **Question 5:** What lifestyle does Paul commend to the Ephesian elders in contrast to coveting silver, gold, and apparel? How does he motivate them to live that way?

Paul cites Jesus in Acts 20 as saying, "It is more blessed to give than to receive." Was that just his way of summarizing and restating what Jesus had already said in Luke 12:33? It certainly seems possible.

[33]Sell your possessions, and give to the needy. Provide yourselves with moneybags that do not grow old, with a treasure in the heavens that does not fail, where no thief approaches and no moth destroys.

Question 6: According to this verse, how does Jesus consider it "more blessed to give than to receive"? What does it cost to have "a treasure in the heavens"?

DAY 4—THE POWER TO PERSEVERE

Toward the end of his letter, knowing their need to press on in faith and good works, the author of Hebrews encourages his readers by reminding them of their past obedience. Observe what he says:

[32]But recall the former days when, after you were enlightened, you endured a hard struggle with sufferings, [33]sometimes being publicly exposed to reproach and affliction, and sometimes being partners with those so treated. [34]For you had compassion on those in prison, and you joyfully accepted the plundering of your property, since you knew that you yourselves had a better possession and an abiding one. [35]Therefore do not throw away your confidence, which has a great reward. (10:32–35)

* Question 7: What evidences of love do you see in this passage? Do you see anything "Christian hedonistic" about it?

Another way to find encouragement to persevere is not only by remembering your own obedience but also by looking at the obedience of others and considering its outcome.

Listen to what the author of Hebrews says about Moses:

> ²⁴By faith Moses, when he was grown up, refused to be called the
> son of Pharaoh's daughter, ²⁵choosing rather to be mistreated
> with the people of God than to enjoy the fleeting pleasures of sin.
> ²⁶He considered the reproach of Christ greater wealth than the
> treasures of Egypt, for he was looking to the reward. (11:24–26)

Question 8: Why was Moses persuaded to join the Hebrews rather than to stay in Pharaoh's palace? What did it cost him?

Day 5—Suffering for Love and Joy

Moses loved the people of God and laid down his life for them, because he saw the rewards of God to be far greater than the "fleeting pleasures of sin." The author of Hebrews calls his suffering "the reproach of Christ" (11:26), because Christ also suffered by being mistreated for the good of others. But was Christ's motivation different than Moses'?

> ¹Therefore, since we are surrounded by so great a cloud of
> witnesses, let us also lay aside every weight, and sin which clings
> so closely, and let us run with endurance the race that is set before
> us, ²looking to Jesus, the founder and perfecter of our faith, who
> for the joy that was set before him endured the cross, despising
> the shame, and is seated at the right hand of the throne of God.
> (Hebrews 12:1–2)

* **Question 9:** What does the author say compelled Jesus to endure the cross? What joy was he anticipating?

Christ's life was the perfect example of obedience. Therefore the author of Hebrews draws his letter to a close by calling the readers, who have already been redeemed by his blood, to now live like their Savior did.

> [12]So Jesus also suffered outside the gate in order to sanctify the people through his own blood. [13]Therefore let us go to him outside the camp and bear the reproach he endured. [14]For here we have no lasting city, but we seek the city that is to come. (13:12–14)

Question 10: How might our enduring reproach, like Christ's, benefit other people? What threatens to hinder you from living like he did?

FURTHER UP AND FURTHER IN

Read or listen to "Love: The Labor of Christian Hedonism," an online sermon at the Desiring God Web site.

Question 11: What is Piper trying to prove in this sermon? Do you agree with his conclusion? Explain.

Question 12: How does Piper define love? What does he say is *not* love?

Question 13: How does Piper answer the potential objections from 1 Corinthians 10:24 and 13:5 and Romans 15:1–3 to Christian hedonism's understanding of love?

Read the article "Dissatisfied Contentment" on the Desiring God Web site.

Question 14: After thinking through the vertical dimension of Christian hedonism, how did Piper come to view the ideal Christian life?

Question 15: How did Piper later qualify this view? In other words, how does he define "dissatisfied contentment"?

─→ *While You Watch the DVD, Take Notes* ←─

Argument 8: Love for People Is the _____ and _____ of Joy in God

What worried Piper about vertical Christian hedonism in the early days?

Where does love come from in the Christian life?

How does Piper respond to the suggestion that he emphasize pursuing obedience instead of emphasizing pursuing happiness?

Why does Piper not consider himself an ideal lover of people?

—◆ *After You Watch the DVD, Discuss What You've Learned* ◆—

1. Have you ever felt offended because someone found pleasure in doing something good for you? Why or why not? Now flip the question around: Have you ever felt offended because someone did *not* find pleasure in doing something good for you? Why or why not?

2. Think of a difficult relationship in your life or one that is currently not going as well as you would like. What are some ways that your behavior toward this person might become more loving? How would this relate to your satisfaction in God?

3. If loving others leads to increased joy in God, why do you think the Scriptures must repeatedly remind believers to love one another (see 1 Thessalonians 4:9–10; Hebrews 10:24; 1 Peter 1:22; 1 John 4:7; etc.)?

—* *After You Discuss, Make Application* *—

1. What was the most meaningful part of this lesson for you? Was there a sentence, concept, or idea that really struck you? Why? Record your thoughts in the space below.

2. The apostle John says that we must not love in word or talk only, "but in deed and in truth" (1 John 3:18). Take a moment to pray and ask God if there are any deeds of love that are missing in your life. You may wish to write them below, making a short note beside each one on how it could express and increase your joy in God.

THE GRAND OBLIGATION (PART 4): THE STRENGTH FOR SANCTIFICATION AND SERVICE

A Companion Study to the Desiring God DVD, Session 8

LESSON OBJECTIVES

It is our prayer that after you have finished this lesson…
- You will understand how seeking joy subdues pride and self-pity.
- You will recognize the proper role of self-denial in the Christian life.
- You will see how satisfaction in God enables suffering and service for Christ.

—➤ *Before You Watch the DVD, Study and Prepare* ◄•—

DAY 1—PLEASURE VERSUS PRIDE

Lesson 9 covers the last of the arguments for why it is not only *possible* but also *necessary* for Christians to seek after God by pursuing their joy in him.

John Piper will argue in this lesson's DVD session that self-pity is the form that pride takes in the heart of the weak and wounded. Although it does not outwardly look like the person who boasts in himself, self-pity still involves a sense of entitlement, and that comes from pride.

What does this have to do with Christian hedonism? Let us begin by looking at Mark 10:23–30.

> [23]And Jesus looked around and said to his disciples, "How difficult it will be for those who have wealth to enter the kingdom of God!" [24]And the disciples were amazed at his words. But Jesus said to them again, "Children, how difficult it is to enter the kingdom of God! [25]It is easier for a camel to go through the eye of a needle than for a rich person to enter the kingdom of God." [26]And they were exceedingly astonished, and said to him, "Then who can be saved?" [27]Jesus looked at them and said, "With man it is impossible, but not with God. For all things are possible with God." [28]Peter began to say to him, "See, we have left everything and followed you." [29]Jesus said, "Truly, I say to you, there is no one who has left house or brothers or sisters or mother or father or children or lands, for my sake and for the gospel, [30]who will not receive a hundredfold now in this time, houses and brothers and sisters and mothers and children and lands, with persecutions, and in the age to come eternal life.

* **Question 1:** From what you see in this passage, why do you think Jesus responded to Peter the way that he did? What effect do you think Jesus' response had on him?

The alternate manifestation of pride is, of course, boasting. This form of pride is a temptation especially for those who are highly esteemed by others. Observe how the great pioneer missionary to Africa, David Livingstone, handled the praise of men.

> For my own part, I have never ceased to rejoice that God has appointed me to such an office. People talk of the sacrifice I have made in spending so much of my life in Africa.... Is that a sacrifice which brings its own blest reward in healthful activity, the consciousness of doing good, peace of mind, and a bright hope of a glorious destiny hereafter? Away with the word in such a view, and with such a thought! It is emphatically no sacrifice. Say rather it is a privilege. Anxiety, sickness, suffering, or danger, now and then, with a foregoing of the common conveniences and charities of this life, may make us pause, and cause the spirit to waver, and the soul to sink; but let this only be for a moment. All these are nothing when compared with the glory which shall be revealed in and for us. I never made a sacrifice.[22]

Question 2: How did David Livingstone feel about his calling? Why does he deny the notion that he had made such a great sacrifice?

Day 2—The Purpose of Self-Denial

On the face of it, by calling people to pursue maximum personal fulfillment, Christian hedonism appears to go entirely against Jesus Christ's call for his followers to deny themselves.

[34]And calling the crowd to him with his disciples, he said to them, "If anyone would come after me, let him deny himself and take up his cross and follow me. [35]For whoever would save his life will lose it, but whoever loses his life for my sake and the gospel's will save it." (Mark 8:34–35)

* **Question 3:** What does Jesus say is required of those who would follow him? How does he try to motivate the people to fulfill this requirement?

Jesus brings up the issue of self-denial elsewhere in the Gospels, in a parable about the kingdom of heaven.

[45]Again, the kingdom of heaven is like a merchant in search of fine pearls, [46]who, on finding one pearl of great value, went and sold all that he had and bought it. (Matthew 13:45–46)

Question 4: What does this parable teach you about self-denial?

The New Testament has lots to say about self-denial, but not about self-denial as an end in itself. We are told to deny ourselves and to take up our crosses in order that we may follow Christ; and nearly every description of what we shall ultimately find if we do so contains an appeal to desire.[23]

Day 3—The Strength to Endure

Another argument for the necessity of Christian hedonism says that striving for joy is what sustains Christian suffering.

Jesus talks about suffering at the end of the Beatitudes:

> [10]Blessed are those who are persecuted for righteousness' sake, for theirs is the kingdom of heaven. [11]Blessed are you when others revile you and persecute you and utter all kinds of evil against you falsely on my account. [12]Rejoice and be glad, for your reward is great in heaven, for so they persecuted the prophets who were before you. (Matthew 5:10–12)

* **Question 5:** According to this passage, how should a person respond to lies, insults, and persecutions? What enables this kind of response?

Paul likewise speaks about Christian suffering:

> [16]So we do not lose heart. Though our outer self is wasting away, our inner self is being renewed day by day. [17]For this light momentary affliction is preparing for us an eternal weight of glory beyond all comparison, [18]as we look not to the things that are seen but to the things that are unseen. For the things that are seen are transient, but the things that are unseen are eternal. (2 Corinthians 4:16–18)

Question 6: What reason does Paul give for why he doesn't lose heart? What does he do to endure?

Day 4—Do Your Duty

Christian hedonism does not deny that duty is a part of the Christian life. It simply affirms that one of our duties is to "Rejoice in the Lord *always*" (Philippians 4:4). This raises the question, then, of how rejoicing in God can and should be done in the midst of all our other duties.

Take a look at how Peter speaks about our duty to serve others.

> [10]As each has received a gift, use it to serve one another, as good stewards of God's varied grace: [11]whoever speaks, as one who speaks oracles of God; whoever serves, as one who serves by the strength that God supplies—in order that in everything God may be glorified through Jesus Christ. To him belong glory and dominion forever and ever. Amen. (1 Peter 4:10–11)

* **Question 7:** List as many observations as you can from this passage about Christian service. How might joy be involved? How does our service glorify God? Service to others is, in the end, service to God. There are places in Scripture, however, where we are commanded to serve God more directly.

> [12]If I were hungry, I would not tell you, for the world and its fullness are mine. [13]Do I eat the flesh of bulls or drink the blood of goats? [14]Offer to God a sacrifice of thanksgiving, and perform your vows to the Most High, [15]and call upon me in the day of trouble; I will deliver you, and you shall glorify me. (Psalm 50:12–15)

Question 8: What are some of the ways we should serve God, according to this psalm? How does he get glory here?

Day 5—The Duty of Dependence

The question about how joy relates to our other Christian duties is worth considering a little further. Read these last two verses, one from the prophet Isaiah and one from 2 Chronicles.

> [4]From of old no one has heard or perceived by the ear, no eye has seen a God besides you, who acts for those who wait for him. (Isaiah 64:4)

* **Question 9:** What does this verse say is unique to the God of Israel? What implications does this attribute have for his people?

> [9]For the eyes of the LORD run to and fro throughout the whole earth, to give strong support to those whose heart is blameless toward him. (2 Chronicles 16:9)

Question 10: What does it suggest that "the eyes of the LORD run to and fro"? What must a person do to gain his support?

Further Up and Further In

Read or listen to "It's My Pleasure!" an online sermon at the Desiring God Web site.

Question 11: Why, according to Piper, is humility so important?

Question 12: How does he describe a person who is humble?

Question 13: How does Christian hedonism aid humility and hinder pride?

Read the article "Brothers, Tell Them Not to Serve God!" on the Desiring God Web site.

Question 14: What does Piper say is the difference between Uncle Sam and Jesus Christ?

Question 15: How is serving God similar to serving money? What will true service to God entail?

→✺ *While You Watch the DVD, Take Notes* ✺←

Argument 9: Pride and Self-Pity Are _____ by
the Pursuit of Joy in God

What common phrase illustrates the way Christian hedonism
deflects pride?

Argument 10: There Is Self-Denial, but All for the Sake of Ultimate Satisfaction in God

What did Ayn Rand falsely conclude about the Christian life?

Argument 11: Suffering Is _____ and
_____ by the Pursuit of Joy in God

What does Piper see as the key to enduring suffering?

What makes a Christian "salty"?

Argument 12: The Duty of Serving God Is _____
    by the Joy of Being _____ by God

What is the key to serving God?

→ *After You Watch the DVD, Discuss What You've Learned* ←

1. "Christian hedonism says we should secure our joy by avoiding
    activities that could tempt us to become proud." True or false?
    Explain your answer.

2. Have you ever received greater joy after having denied yourself
    something first? Share your experience with the group. What
    compelled you to deny yourself, and what enabled you to carry
    it through?

3. Why is it dangerous to perform duties when you aren't looking for God to serve you in the process? Are there any duties that you are tempted to perform like this?

—❖ *After You Discuss, Make Application* ❖—

1. What was the most meaningful part of this lesson for you? Was there a sentence, concept, or idea that really struck you? Why? Record your thoughts in the space below.

2. In what area of your life do you need more self-denial? That is, where are you settling for mud pies when you could be moving closer to the salty air of satisfaction in God? Write down one area, listing next to it all of the promises of God you can think of that would empower you to deny yourself, along with any practical ideas.

HOW THEN SHALL WE FIGHT FOR JOY? (PART 1): KNOW ITS SOURCES AND SETBACKS

A Companion Study to the Desiring God *DVD, Session 9*

LESSON OBJECTIVES

It is our prayer that after you have finished this lesson…
- You will understand that joy is ultimately a gift from God, but one that we must also fight for.
- You will learn how to reverse the joy-stealing effects of sin.
- You will recognize the incredible power of Scripture in the fight for joy.

—❋ *Before You Watch the DVD, Study and Prepare* ❋—

DAY 1—KNOW YOUR SOURCES

If the last four lessons are right, and we are convinced that delighting in God is the duty of every Christian, then it now remains for us to consider *how* to delight in him. Because, as we learned in Lesson 6, as sinners we do not always delight in God as we ought.

This lesson will introduce us to some of what Scripture teaches about how we can grow in our enjoyment of God.

> [22]But the fruit of the Spirit is love, joy, peace, patience, kindness, goodness, faithfulness, [23]gentleness, self-control; against such things there is no law. (Galatians 5:22–23)

* **Question 1:** What do these verses tell us about how a person gets joy? Why do you think God has arranged it this way?

Now look at 2 Corinthians 1:24 and 1 Timothy 6:12:

> [24]Not that we lord it over your faith, but we work with you for your joy, for you stand firm in your faith.

> [12]Fight the good fight of the faith. Take hold of the eternal life to which you were called and about which you made the good confession in the presence of many witnesses.

Question 2: What do these verses teach us about how to get joy? Are they at odds with Galatians 5:22? Why or why not?

Day 2—Respond to Sin

In the previous section we saw that joy is a fruit of the Spirit (Galatians 5:22). Paul also informs us in Galatians that there is an enemy to the Spirit's work in us—our flesh: "For the desires of the flesh are against the Spirit, and the desires of the Spirit are against the flesh, for these are opposed to each other, to keep you from doing the things you want to do" (Galatians 5:17).

He highlights this antagonism between the flesh and the Spirit in Romans also:

> [13]For if you live according to the flesh you will die, but if by the
> Spirit you put to death the deeds of the body, you will live. (8:13)

Question 3: What should be our response to the impulses of the flesh, according to Paul? How should this be done?

Our aim should be to slay sin before it gets the best of us. Nonetheless, in this life we are all prone to periodic failures. How can we rejoice even when we have failed? Micah shows us how:

> [8]Rejoice not over me, O my enemy; when I fall, I shall rise;
> when I sit in darkness, the LORD will be a light to me. [9]I will
> bear the indignation of the LORD because I have sinned against
> him, until he pleads my cause and executes judgment for me. He
> will bring me out to the light; I shall look upon his vindication.
> (Micah 7:8–9)

* **Question 4:** How does Micah respond after having sinned? How can he speak so confidently?

DAY 3—SET YOUR AIM

Rather than turning to sin to be satisfied—which will only leave us hungrier in the end—we must turn elsewhere. But what are we looking for? What do we seek to see?

> [3]And even if our gospel is veiled, it is veiled only to those who are perishing. [4]In their case the god of this world has blinded the minds of the unbelievers, to keep them from seeing the light of the gospel of the glory of Christ, who is the image of God. [5]For what we proclaim is not ourselves, but Jesus Christ as Lord, with ourselves as your servants for Jesus' sake. [6]For God, who said, "Let light shine out of darkness," has shone in our hearts to give the light of the knowledge of the glory of God in the face of Jesus Christ. (2 Corinthians 4:3–6)

* **Question 5:** What or where is the source of the light of the gospel? What keeps unbelievers from believing?

What effect does seeing the light of the gospel have on those who can see? Both Paul and John inform us:

¹⁸And we all, with unveiled face, beholding the glory of the Lord, are being transformed into the same image from one degree of glory to another. For this comes from the Lord who is the Spirit. (2 Corinthians 3:18)

²Beloved, we are God's children now, and what we will be has not yet appeared; but we know that when he appears we shall be like him, because we shall see him as he is. (1 John 3:2)

Question 6: What happens when believers look upon the glory of the Lord? Is this something that can be done before his second coming? If yes, how?

Day 4—Wield the Word

How can we behold the face of Christ even though we "have not seen him" and "do not now see him" in the flesh (1 Peter 1:8)? What has God left for us in order that we may see and know and delight in him? Consider what Jesus says in John's gospel:

¹¹These things I have spoken to you, that my joy may be in you, and that your joy may be full. (15:11)

Question 7: What does Jesus say is the purpose behind his words? What implications does this have for those seeking their satisfaction in God?

The Old Testament also tells us about how a person can be happy in God:

> ¹Blessed [Hebrew: "happy"] is the man who walks not in the counsel of the wicked, nor stands in the way of sinners, nor sits in the seat of scoffers; ²but his delight is in the law of the LORD, and on his law he meditates day and night. ³He is like a tree planted by streams of water that yields its fruit in its season, and its leaf does not wither. In all that he does, he prospers. (Psalm 1:1–3)

> * **Question 8:** How does the "blessed" or "happy" man live? What is the result of such a life?

Day 5—Watch Others

Sometimes one of the best ways to find help in our own quest for joy is to learn from those who have gone before us. Hearing about their failures and successes is a way of finding comfort and being challenged in the midst of our own.

Listen to the story of Hudson Taylor, a pioneer missionary to China, and how he sought to live according to Psalm 1 (see Day 4):

> It was not easy for Mr. Taylor, in his changeful life, to make time for prayer and Bible study, but he knew that it was vital. Well do the writers remember traveling with him month after month in northern China, by cart and wheelbarrow with the poorest of inns at night. Often with only one large room for coolies and travelers alike, they would screen off a corner for their father and another for themselves, with curtains of some sort; and then, after

sleep at last had brought a measure of quiet, they would hear a match struck and see the flicker of candlelight which told that Mr. Taylor, however weary, was pouring over the little Bible in two volumes always at hand. From two to four A.M. was the time he usually gave to prayer; the time he could be most sure of being undisturbed to wait upon God.[24]

Question 9: How did Hudson Taylor's life compare to the man of Psalm 1? Why did he live like this?

George Müller, who established and ran orphanages in England with radical dependence upon God, is another helpful example of devotional living.

The point is this: I saw more clearly than ever, that the first great and primary business to which I ought to attend every day was, to have my soul happy in the Lord. The first thing to be concerned about was not, how much I might serve the Lord, how I might glorify the Lord; but how I might get my soul into a happy state, and how my inner man might be nourished. For I might seek to set the truth before the unconverted, I might seek to benefit believers, I might seek to relieve the distressed, I might in other ways seek to behave myself as it becomes a child of God in this world; and yet, not being happy in the Lord, and not being nourished and strengthened in my inner man day by day, all this might not be attended to in a right spirit.[25]

* Question 10: What was the main purpose behind Müller's daily disciplines? Why did he think this was so important?

FURTHER UP AND FURTHER IN

Read or listen to "The Bible: Kindling for Christian Hedonism," an online sermon at the Desiring God Web site.

Question 11: How is Jesus the foundation of Piper's confidence that the Bible is the Word of God?

Question 12: What, according to Piper, does the Bible do to kindle and preserve our joy?

Read the article "How Dead People Do Battle with Sin" on the Desiring God Web site.

Question 13: How does Piper define "the flesh"?

Question 14: What does Piper say is the demand of Romans 8:13? What does this verse *not* mean?

Question 15: Where does temptation get its power? How does faith do battle with it?

--→ *While You Watch the DVD, Take Notes* ←--

How Then Shall We Fight for Joy? Part 1

1. Realize that authentic joy in God is ____ _____.
2. Realize that joy must be _____ _____ relentlessly.
3. Resolve to _____ all known _____ in your life.
4. Learn the secret of _____ guilt—how to fight like a _____ sinner.
5. Realize that the battle is primarily a fight to _____ God for who he is.
6. _____ on the _____ of God day and night.

--→ *After You Watch the DVD, Discuss What You've Learned* ←--

1. How does the fact that joy is a gift affect the way you fight for it? How would it not lead you to become totally passive in the pursuit of joy? Or does it? Explain.

2. Have you ever seen God in Scripture? Think back to a time when God touched your heart through something you saw of him in the Bible, and then share it with the group. What effect did it have on you?

3. What is the greatest hindrance to your time in the Word and in prayer? What has helped you the most?

—➤ *After You Discuss, Make Application* ◀—

1. What was the most meaningful part of this lesson for you? Was there a sentence, concept, or idea that really struck you? Why? Record your thoughts in the space below.

2. How is your devotional life going? Take a moment to do a little assessment:
    How often do you spend time in the Bible and in prayer?
    How long do you spend?
    Where do you do it?
    What are your plans for reading and prayer, if any?
    After reviewing your answers, is there anything you see missing or in need of adjustment? Take another moment to consider and pray about whether things should change and how, and then write it down.

HOW THEN SHALL WE FIGHT FOR JOY? (PART 2): MAKE USE OF THE MEANS OF GRACE

A Companion Study to the Desiring God *DVD, Session 10*

LESSON OBJECTIVES

It is our prayer that after you have finished this lesson…
- You will see how prayer and patience are indispensable means to finding joy in God.
- You will understand the importance of having good fellowship and holy influences in your life.
- You will recognize the very practical, physical components involved in the pursuit of joy.

→ *Before You Watch the DVD, Study and Prepare* ←

DAY 1—ASK FOR IT

This lesson continues looking at the different strategies in Scripture for what we can do to grow our gladness in God.

The psalms provide many examples of how people have fought for joy. Examine these two lines from Psalm 119:

[18]Open my eyes, that I may behold wondrous things out of your law.

[36]Incline my heart to your testimonies, and not to selfish gain!

* **Question 1:** How did the psalmist seek to understand Scripture? How did he combat selfish desires for gain?

Or consider what Moses, speaking on behalf of the people of Israel, says in Psalm 90:

[14]Satisfy us in the morning with your steadfast love, that we may rejoice and be glad all our days.

Question 2: What did the people of Israel seek to see of God through prayer? Why?

DAY 2—TELL YOURSELF HOW IT IS

Asking God in prayer is not the only strategy of the psalmists. Notice what the Sons of Korah do in Psalm 42:

⁵Why are you cast down, O my soul, and why are you in turmoil within me? Hope in God; for I shall again praise him, my salvation ⁶and my God.

Question 3: What do the Sons of Korah model as a way to fight for hope?

Martyn Lloyd-Jones, one of the great preachers of the twentieth century, says in his book *Spiritual Depression:*

Have you realized that most of your unhappiness in life is due to the fact that you are listening to yourself instead of talking to yourself? Take those thoughts that come to you the moment you wake up in the morning. You have not originated them but they are talking to you, they bring back the problems of yesterday, etc. Somebody is talking. Who is talking to you? Your self is talking to you. Now this man's treatment [in Psalm 42] was this: instead of allowing this self to talk to him, he starts talking to himself. "Why art thou cast down, O my soul?" he asks. His soul had been depressing him, crushing him. So he stands up and says: "Self, listen for a moment, I will speak to you."[26]

* **Question 4:** What did Lloyd-Jones see happening in Psalm 42? If you were to follow the psalmist's example, what kinds of things would you preach to yourself?

DAY 3—INVOLVE OTHERS

The fight for joy is often an individual battle, such as when you are praying alone or preaching to yourself. But interaction with other people also plays a strong role in the status of your spiritual health.

The author of Hebrews was well aware of this.

[12]Take care, brothers, lest there be in any of you an evil, unbelieving heart, leading you to fall away from the living God. [13]But exhort one another every day, as long as it is called "today," that none of you may be hardened by the deceitfulness of sin. (3:12–13)

* **Question 5:** What does the author of Hebrews recommend for how to fight against sin? Why does he think this strategy is so necessary?

King Solomon, in the book of Proverbs, also shared his insight into the way others influence our spiritual lives:

[20]Whoever walks with the wise becomes wise, but the companion of fools will suffer harm. (13:20)

Question 6: What is the general principle behind this verse? What does this say about the kind of people that you want to "walk" with? Be specific.

DAY 4—DON'T GIVE UP

There are times when the Lord, in his wisdom, still chooses to withhold joy from us, despite all of our praying, preaching, and fellowshipping with others. These can be very dark and difficult times. What should our behavior be in the midst of them?

> ¹I waited patiently for the LORD; he inclined to me and heard my cry. ²He drew me up from the pit of destruction, out of the miry bog, and set my feet upon a rock, making my steps secure. ³He put a new song in my mouth, a song of praise to our God. Many will see and fear, and put their trust in the LORD. (Psalm 40:1–3)

> * **Question 7:** How did David respond after being placed in the pit of destruction? What effect did his time there have on himself and others?

William Cowper, the eighteenth-century evangelical poet who also struggled with depression most of his life, wrote several great hymns that still serve the church today. One of these hymns is "God Moves in a Mysterious Way."

God moves in a mysterious way
his wonders to perform;
He plants his footsteps in the sea,
and rides upon the storm.

Deep in unfathomable mines
of never failing skill,
He treasures up his bright designs
and works his sovereign will.

You fearful saints, fresh courage take;
the clouds you so much dread
Are big with mercy and shall break
in blessings on your head.

His purposes will ripen fast,
unfolding every hour;
The bud may have a bitter taste,
but sweet will be the flower.

Blind unbelief is sure to err
and scan his work in vain:
God is his own interpreter,
and he will make it plain.

Question 8: What are some of the encouragements Cowper gives
in these lines to suffering saints?

DAY 5—USE YOUR BODY

The interrelationship between the human body and soul is real and pro-
found. Any individuals who have ever gone a night without sleep knows
that their soul is not the same the next day. Knowing this, how can we
use our bodies in ways that serve our souls?

Take a look at these two verses from Psalm 127.

[1]Unless the LORD builds the house, they labor in vain who build
it; unless the LORD guards the city, the watchman keeps awake in

vain. ²It is vain for you to rise up early, to retire late, to eat the bread of painful labors; for He gives to His beloved even in his sleep. (Psalm 127:1–2, NASB)

* **Question 9:** What do work and rest patterns signify about a person's soul? According to these verses, how does a person receive grace from the Lord?

This story from the life of Elijah illustrates that sleep is not the only physical help in fighting for joy.

¹Ahab told Jezebel all that Elijah had done, and how he had killed all the prophets with the sword. ²Then Jezebel sent a messenger to Elijah, saying, "So may the gods do to me and more also, if I do not make your life as the life of one of them by this time tomorrow." ³Then he was afraid, and he arose and ran for his life and came to Beersheba, which belongs to Judah, and left his servant there.
⁴But he himself went a day's journey into the wilderness and came and sat down under a broom tree. And he asked that he might die, saying, "It is enough; now, O LORD, take away my life, for I am no better than my fathers." ⁵And he lay down and slept under a broom tree. And behold, an angel touched him and said to him, "Arise and eat." ⁶And he looked, and behold, there was at his head a cake baked on hot stones and a jar of water. And he ate and drank and lay down again. ⁷And the angel of the LORD came again a second time and touched him and said, "Arise and eat, for the journey is too great for you." ⁸And he arose and ate and drank,

and went in the strength of that food forty days and forty nights
to Horeb, the mount of God. (1 Kings 19:1–8)

Question 10: How did the angel of the Lord minister to Elijah?
What effect did it have on him?

Further Up and Further In

**Read or listen to "Prayer: The Power of Christian Hedonism," an
online sermon at the Desiring God Web site.**

Question 11: Why, according to Piper, will Christian hedonists
"above all be people of prayer"?

Question 12: In your own words, how does he answer the question "How is God glorified by prayer?"

Question 13: What two reasons does he give for why prayer leads
to fullness of joy?

Read the article "Clusters of Hope" on the Desiring God Web site.

> **Question 14:** According to Piper, what are some reasons we do not find hope?

> **Question 15:** What tasks does he propose for going hard after hope?

--» *While You Watch the DVD, Take Notes* «--

How Then Shall We Fight for Joy? Part 2

7. _____ earnestly and continually for open heart eyes and an _____ for God.

8. Learn to _____ to yourself rather than _____ to yourself.

9. Spend time with _____ people who help you _____ God and _____ the fight.

10. Be _____ in the night of God's seeming absence.

11. Get the _____, _____, and _____ _____ that your body was designed by God to have.

12. Make a proper use of God's revelation in _____.

13. Read great books about _____ and biographies of _____ _____.

14. Do the _____ and _____ thing for the sake of others.

15. Get a _____ _____ for the cause of Christ and pour yourself into the _____.

--→ *After You Watch the DVD, Discuss What You've Learned* ←--

1. Have you ever preached to yourself? What kinds of thoughts did you have to overcome? What truths or promises did you respond with?

2. Do you have a friend like Jonathan who strengthens your hands in the Lord? If so, how does he or she do that? How can you be a friend like this to others?

3. What patterns of exercise, rest, and diet do you find most healthy and helpful for your soul? What enables you to maintain these patterns? What keeps you from them?

→ *After You Discuss, Make Application* ←

1. What was the most meaningful part of this lesson for you? Was there a sentence, concept, or idea that really struck you? Why? Record your thoughts in the space below.

2. In Lesson 5 we encouraged you to memorize a verse, but do you have an ongoing plan for memorizing Scripture? Several of the strategies covered in the past two lessons have highlighted the powerful place of memorized Scripture in the fight for joy. Take some time either to consider a new plan or to assess your old plan, and then set goals to memorize key verses. One plan that you may find helpful is the Fighter Verse Program, which you can find by searching "fighter verses" on the Desiring God Web site.

REVIEW AND CONCLUSION

LESSON OBJECTIVES

It is our prayer that after you have finished this lesson…
- You will be able to summarize and synthesize what you've learned.
- You will hear what others in your group have learned.
- You will be encouraged to press on together in enjoying God more and sharing that joy with others.

WHAT HAVE YOU LEARNED?

There are no study questions to answer in preparation for this lesson. Instead, spend your time writing a few paragraphs that explain what you've learned in this group study. To help you do this, you may choose to review the notes you've taken in the previous lessons. Then, after you've written down what you've learned, write down some questions that still remain in your mind about anything addressed in these lessons. Be prepared to share these reflections and questions with the group in the next lesson.

NOTES

Use this space to record anything in the group discussion that you want to remember:

LEADER'S GUIDE

As the leader of this group study, it is imperative that you are completely familiar with this study guide and the *Desiring God* DVD set. Therefore, it is our strong recommendation that you (1) read and understand the introduction, (2) that you skim each lesson, surveying its layout and content, and (3) that you read the entire Leader's Guide before you begin the group study and distribute the study guides.

BEFORE LESSON 1

Before the first lesson, you will need to know approximately how many participants you will have in your group study. Each participant will need his or her own study guide! Therefore, be sure to order enough study guides. You will distribute these study guides at the beginning of the first lesson.

It is also our strong recommendation that you, as the leader, familiarize yourself with this study guide and the *Desiring God* DVD set in order to answer any questions that might arise and also to ensure that each group session runs smoothly and maximizes the learning of the participants. It is not necessary for you to preview *Desiring God* in its entirety—although it certainly wouldn't hurt!—but you should be prepared to navigate your way through each DVD menu.

DURING LESSON 1

Each lesson is designed for a one-hour group session. Lessons 2–12 require preparatory work from the participants before this group session. Lesson 1, however, requires no preparation on the part of the participants.

The following schedule is how we suggest that you use the first hour of your group study:

Introduction to the Study Guide (10 minutes)

Introduce this study guide and the *Desiring God* DVD. Share with the group why you chose to lead the group study using these resources. Inform your group of the commitment that this study will require and motivate them to work hard. Pray for the twelve-week study, asking God for the grace you will need. Then distribute one study guide to each participant. You may read the introduction aloud if you want, or you may immediately turn the group to Lesson 1.

Personal Introductions (15 minutes)

Since group discussion will be an integral part of this guided study, it is crucial that each participant feels welcome and safe. The goal of each lesson is for every participant to contribute to the discussion in some way. Therefore, during these fifteen minutes, have the participants introduce themselves. You may choose to use the questions listed in the section entitled "About Yourself," or you may ask questions of your own choosing.

Discussion (25 minutes)

Transition from the time of introductions to the discussion questions listed under the heading "A Preview of *Desiring God*." Invite everyone in the class to respond to these questions, but don't let the discussion become too involved. These questions are designed to spark interest and generate questions. The aim is not to come to definitive answers yet.

Review and Closing (10 minutes)

End the group session by previewing Lesson 2 with the group participants and informing them of the preparation they must do before the group meets again. Encourage them to be faithful in preparing for the next lesson. Answer any questions that the group may have and then close in prayer.

BEFORE LESSONS 2–11

As the group leader, you should do all the preparation for each lesson that is required of the group participants, namely, the ten study questions.

Furthermore, it is highly recommended that you complete the entire "Further Up and Further In" section. This is not required of the group participants, but it will enrich your preparation and help you to guide and shape the conversation more effectively.

The group leader should also preview the session of *Desiring God* that will be covered in the next lesson. So, for example, if the group participants are doing the preparatory work for Lesson 3, you should preview *Desiring God*, Session 2 before the group meets and views it. Previewing each session will better equip you to understand the material and answer questions. If you want to pause the DVD in the midst of the session in order to clarify or discuss, previewing the session will allow you to plan where you want to take your pauses.

Finally, you may want to supplement or modify the discussion questions or the application assignment. Please remember that **this study guide is a resource**; any additions or changes you make that better match the study to your particular group are encouraged. This study guide should function as a helpful tool and *resource*. As the group leader, your own discernment, creativity, and guidance are invaluable, and you should adapt the material as you see fit.

Plan for about two hours of your own preparation before each lesson!

DURING LESSONS 2–11

Again, let us stress that during Lessons 2–11 you may use the group time in whatever way you desire. The following schedule, however, is what we suggest:

Discussion (10 minutes)

Begin your time with prayer. The tone you set in your prayer will likely be impressed upon the group participants: if your prayer is serious and heartfelt, the group participants will be serious about prayer; if your prayer is hasty, sloppy, or a token gesture, the group participants will share this same attitude toward prayer. So model the kind of praying that you desire your students to imitate. Remember, the blood of Jesus has bought your access to the throne of grace.

After praying, review the preparatory work that the participants completed. How did they answer the questions? Which questions did they find to be the most interesting or the most confusing? What observations or insights can they share with the group? If you would like to review some tips for leading productive discussions, please turn to Appendix B at the end of this study guide.

The group participants will be provided an opportunity to apply what they've learned in Lessons 2–11. As the group leader, you can choose whether it would be appropriate for the group to discuss these assignments during this ten-minute time slot.

DVD Viewing (30 minutes)[27]

Play the session from the *Desiring God* DVD set that corresponds to the lesson you're studying. You may choose to pause the DVD at crucial points to check for understanding and provide clarification. Or you may choose to watch the DVD without interruption.

Discussion and Closing (20 minutes)

Foster discussion on what was taught during John Piper's session. You may do this by first reviewing the DVD notes (under the heading "While You Watch the DVD, Take Notes") and then proceeding to the discussion questions (under the heading "After You Watch the DVD, Discuss What You've Learned"). These discussion questions are meant to be springboards that launch the group into further and deeper discussion. Don't feel limited to these questions if the group discussion begins to move in other helpful directions.

Close the time by briefly reviewing the application section and the homework that is expected for the next lesson. Pray and dismiss.

BEFORE LESSON 12

It is important that you encourage the group participants to complete the preparatory work for Lesson 12. This assignment invites the participants to reflect on what they've learned and what remaining questions they still have. As the group leader, this would be a helpful assignment for you to complete as well. In addition, you may want to write down the key concepts of this DVD series that you want the group participants to walk away with.

DURING LESSON 12

The group participants are expected to complete a reflection exercise as part of their preparation for Lesson 12. The bulk of the group time during this last lesson should be focused on reviewing and synthesizing what was learned. Encourage each participant to share some of his or her recorded thoughts. Attempt to answer any remaining questions that they might have.

To close this last lesson, you might want to spend extended time in prayer. If appropriate, take prayer requests relating to what the participants have learned in these twelve weeks and bring these requests to God.

It would be appropriate for you, the group leader, to give a final charge or word of exhortation to end this group study. Speak from your heart and out of the overflow of joy that you have in God.

As a group leader, please receive our blessing as you use this study guide:

> *The LORD bless you and keep you; the LORD make his*
> *face to shine upon you and be gracious to you; the LORD*
> *lift up his countenance upon you and give you peace.*
> *(Numbers 6:24–26)*

APPENDIX A:
SIX-SESSION
INTENSIVE OPTION

We understand that there are circumstances that may prohibit a group from devoting twelve sessions to this study. In view of this, we have designed a six-session intensive option for groups that need to complete the material in less time. In the intensive option, the group should meet for two hours each week. Here is our suggestion for how to complete the material in six weeks:

Week 1   Introduction to the Study Guide and Lesson 1
Week 2   Lessons 2 and 3 (DVD Sessions 1 and 2)
Week 3   Lessons 4 and 5 (DVD Sessions 3 and 4)
Week 4   Lessons 6 and 7 (DVD Sessions 5 and 6)
Week 5   Lessons 8 and 9 (DVD Sessions 7 and 8)
Week 6   Lessons 10 and 11 (DVD Sessions 9 and 10)

Notice that we have not included Lesson 12 in the intensive option. Moreover, because each participant is required to complete two lessons per week, it will be necessary to combine the number of "days" within each lesson so that all of the material is covered. Thus, for example, during Week 2 in the intensive option, each participant will complete:

- Lesson 2, Days 1 and 2, on the first day
- Lesson 2, Days 3 and 4, on the second day
- Lesson 2, Day 5 and Lesson 3, Day 1, on the third day
- Lesson 3, Days 2 and 3, on the fourth day
- Lesson 3, Days 4 and 5, on the fifth day

Because of the amount of material, we recommend that students focus on questions marked with an asterisk (*) first and then, if time permits, complete the rest of the questions.

APPENDIX B:
LEADING PRODUCTIVE
DISCUSSIONS

Note: This material has been adapted from curricula produced by the Bethlehem Institute (TBI), a ministry of Bethlehem Baptist Church. It is used by permission.

It is our conviction that the best group leaders foster an environment in their group that engages the participants. Most people learn by solving problems or by working through things that provoke curiosity or concern. Therefore, we discourage you from ever lecturing for the entire lesson. Although a group leader will constantly shape conversation, clarifying and correcting as needed, he or she will probably not talk for the majority of the lesson. This study guide is meant to facilitate an investigation into biblical truth—an investigation that is shared by the group leader and the participants. Therefore, we encourage you to adopt the posture of a fellow learner who invites participation from everyone in the group.

It might surprise you how eager people can be to share what they have learned in preparing for each lesson. Therefore, you should invite participation by asking your group participants to share their discoveries. Here are some of our tips on facilitating discussion that is engaging and helpful:

- Don't be uncomfortable with an initial silence. Once the first participant shares his or her response, others will be likely to join in. But if you cut the silence short by prompting them, then they are more likely to wait for you to prompt them every time.

- Affirm every answer, if possible, and draw out the participants by asking for clarification. Your aim is to make them feel comfortable sharing their ideas and learning, so be extremely hesitant to shut down a group member's contribution or trump it with your own. This does not mean, however, that you shouldn't correct false ideas—but do it in a spirit of gentleness and love.
- Don't allow a single person or group of persons to dominate the discussion. Involve everyone, if possible, and intentionally invite participation from those who are more reserved or hesitant.
- Labor to show the significance of their study. Emphasize the things that the participants could not have learned without doing the homework.
- Avoid talking too much. The group leader should not monopolize the discussion, but rather guide and shape it. If the group leader does the majority of the talking, the participants will be less likely to interact and engage, and therefore they will not learn as much. Avoid constantly adding the definitive last word.
- The group leader should feel the freedom to linger on a topic or question if the group demonstrates interest. The group leader should also pursue digressions that are helpful and relevant. There is a balance to this, however. The group leader *should* attempt to cover the material. So avoid the extreme of constantly wandering off topic, but also avoid the extreme of limiting the conversation in a way that squelches curiosity or learning.
- The group leader's passion, or lack of it, is infectious. Therefore, if you demonstrate little enthusiasm for the material, it is almost inevitable that your participants will likewise be bored. But if you have a genuine excitement for what you are studying, and if you truly think Bible study is

worthwhile, then your group will be impacted positively. Therefore, it is our recommendation that before you come to the group, you spend enough time working through the homework and praying, so that you can overflow with genuine enthusiasm for the Bible and for God in your group. This point cannot be stressed enough. Delight yourself in God and in his Word!

NOTES

1. Although this resource is designed to be used in a group setting, it can also be used by independent learners. Such learners would have to decide for themselves how to use this resource in the most beneficial way. We would suggest doing everything but the group discussion, if possible.
2. Thirty minutes is only an approximation. Some sessions are longer; others are shorter.
3. Questions marked with an asterisk (*) are questions that we deem to be particularly significant. If your group is completing this study using the six-session intensive option, we recommend that you complete these questions first and then, if time permits, complete the remaining questions. For more information, see Appendix A, "Six-Session Intensive Option."
4. Notice the similarity between this verse and the Westminster Shorter Catechism's answer from Day 1, that the chief end of man is "*to glorify God,* and to enjoy him forever."
5. C. S. Lewis, as quoted in John Piper, *Desiring God,* rev. ed. (Colorado Springs, CO: Multnomah, 2011), 20.
6. Flannery O'Connor, as quoted in Piper, *Desiring God,* 101.
7. John Piper, "The Happiness of God: Foundation for Christian Hedonism," September 11, 1983, www.desiringgod.org/ResourceLibrary/Sermons/ByDate/1983/404_The_Happiness_of_God_Foundation_for_Christian_Hedonism.
8. Piper, *Desiring God,* 32.
9. Piper, *Desiring God,* 41.
10. See, e.g., "Biblical Texts to Show God's Zeal for His Own Glory," November 24, 2007, www.desiringgod.org/ResourceLibrary/

Articles/ByDate/2007/2510_Biblical_Texts_to_Show_Gods_
Zeal_for_His_Glory.

11. Piper, *Desiring God,* 25th Anniversary Reference Edition, 313.
This material also appears in the 1986, 1996, and 2003 editions
of *Desiring God.*

12. Piper, *Desiring God,* 47.

13. Piper, *Desiring God,* 43–44.

14. For a much fuller consideration of the supremacy of God in his
own affections and of his purpose in creating the universe, see
John Piper, *God's Passion for His Glory: Living the Vision of
Jonathan Edwards* (Wheaton, IL: Crossway, 1998), which is
available for purchase or as a free download at www.desiringgod.
org/ResourceLibrary/OnlineBooks/ByTitle/1595_Gods_Passion_
for_His_Glory.

15. John Piper, *Let the Nations Be Glad,* 2nd ed. (Grand Rapids, MI:
Baker Academic, 2003), 21.

16. Piper, *Desiring God,* 48.

17. Piper, *Desiring God,* 49–50.

18. C. S. Lewis, as quoted in Piper, *Desiring God,* 49.

19. Jonathan Edwards, as quoted in Piper, *Desiring God,* 22.

20. C. S. Lewis, as quoted in Piper, *Desiring God,* 99.

21. Edward John Carnell, as quoted in Piper, *Desiring God,* 93.

22. David Livingstone, as quoted in Piper, *Desiring God,* 243.

23. C. S. Lewis, as quoted in Piper, *Desiring God,* 20.

24. Dr. and Mrs. Howard Taylor, as quoted in Piper, *Desiring God,*
151–52.

25. George Müller, as quoted in Piper, *Desiring God,* 155.

26. Martyn Lloyd-Jones, as quoted in Piper, "Learn to Preach
to Yourself Rather Than Listen to Yourself," http://www
.desiringgod.org/resource-library/seminars/desiring-god-part-1.
This material also appears in John Piper, *Desiring God,* 25th
Anniversary Reference Edition, 375, as well as the 2003 edition
of *Desiring God,* 358.

27. Thirty minutes is only an approximation. Some of the sessions are shorter and some are longer. You may need to budget your group time differently, depending upon which session you are viewing.